To Stephen & Brendh –
for the love of the game!

SMART, WRONG, AND LUCKY

The Origin Stories of Baseball's
Unexpected Stars

Jonathan Mayo

TRIUMPH
B O O K S

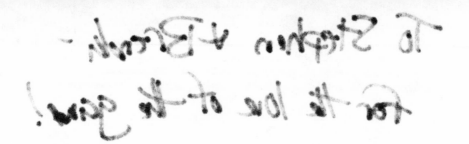

Library of Congress Cataloging-in-Publication Data available upon request.

This book is available in quantity at special discounts for your group or organization. For further information, contact:

Triumph Books LLC
814 North Franklin Street
Chicago, Illinois 60610
(312) 337-0747
www.triumphbooks.com

Printed in U.S.A.
ISBN: 978-1-62937-898-5
Design by Nord Compo

For Ziv and Elena,
whose kindness, resilience, and humor
make my world a better place

Contents

Foreword

Jonathan provides you with insight into the complex world of amateur scouting. Due to Jonathan's baseball knowledge and connections in the game, you can learn details about the signings of some of the best players in recent Major League Baseball history, and back-room knowledge that is not available to the general public. You will gain information from the player's, scout's, and front office's perspectives, along with how difficult it is to scout, draft, and eventually sign a player.

This book focuses on some of the uncovered gems in our game. It is not always the top draft choices that make great players, but individuals that are selected lower in the draft. There is a unique story in each and every signing. The debates—and sometimes arguments—that occur between area scouts, cross checkers, and scouting directors that can alter a franchise's future are captured in each chapter's unique story. How some players that become our game's greatest players, yet fall to being selected in the later rounds of the draft are mesmerizing stories that are rarely unveiled.

Read and enjoy this rare opportunity. You will not be able to put this book down!

—Dave Dombrowski
President, Baseball Operations
Philadelphia Phillies
December 2022

Introduction

In my early days of covering the draft for MLB.com, I was fortunate enough to see and talk to some future first-round picks. In 2004, I spent a lot of time in my hometown of Pittsburgh with Neil Walker, who went on to have a solid big league career. I also traveled to Virginia to see a pair of top college pitching prospects face each other. One of them, Justin Verlander is headed to the Hall of Fame. The other, Justin Orenduff, never made it to the big leagues because of injuries.

A year prior, I drove to eastern Pennsylvania to see a high school outfielder who hit several homers in a doubleheader and ended up being the No. 5 overall pick in the 2003 Draft. Chris Lubanski made it as high as Triple-A and was out of baseball after the 2011 season.

I bring these examples up not to criticize "misses," but rather to show just how hard it is to evaluate amateur players and project who is going to be a big leaguer, let alone a star. Scouts are the foundation of baseball and it is grossly underestimated just how hard they work and how inexact a science it is to find the national pastime's future.

It's often our storytellers who are the true bedrock of our society, and that's definitely true in the baseball ecosystem. No one spins a yarn as well as a scout. And not in a "look at how great I am" way. Sure, any scout will proudly talk about successes, but nearly every one I've talked to has been just as likely to wax eloquent on the ones who got away, or ones they got wrong.

And when given the chance to do a little self-promotion, scouts won't typically go to the first-rounders they signed, though they're no doubt proud of them. Instead, they'll puff their chests out more about the guy they got in the eighth round or the 17th round or beyond. Why? Because in those cases, it was their belief in a player, more than anyone else's, that got that player drafted and gave him the chance to show what he could do in pro ball.

As the draft wears on, decisions fall to the area scouts, the people who cover each region of the map and are responsible for sending in reports on players worthy of consideration. The general manager might see potential first-round picks, the scouting director might only have time to see players in the first several rounds, and even the national and regional cross-checkers only have so many days to see as many players as possible. Even if they got to see a late-round candidate, it's often the conviction of the area scout that is the deciding factor.

And that's what this book is about, those stories of later-round selections who take the opportunity given to them, run with it, and far exceed the expectations of someone taken deep in the draft. The players obviously deserve a ton of credit for the work they put in to become major league stars, and their voices are reflected in each chapter.

But these are really origin stories I wanted to tell, shining a spotlight on the tireless—and often thankless—efforts of the scouts that continue to build this game we love so much. I conducted dozens of interviews with these architects and gave them the floor, allowing them to tell their stories about some of their favorite "finds."

In each case, I afforded the scouts responsible for the discoveries of these stars the opportunity to shout from the rooftops that they knew all along that their guy would be a Cy Young winner, an MVP, an All-Star, a future Hall of Famer. But they're all too smart and know this game is far too humbling. Nary a one took the bait. They might take credit for seeing something that others didn't, but none of them would claim being the Nostradamus of the scouting industry.

So while their humility stands out, I'll be the one to trumpet these accomplishments (while certainly not underselling the work ethics of the players' accomplishments on the field). The scouts responsible for signing each subject in this book all saw something that others didn't see. Perhaps there was some luck working in their favor, but as the saying goes, "Luck is a matter of preparation meeting opportunity."

That 2003 Draft, where Chris Lubanski went No. 5 overall? The career leader in WAR (Wins Above Replacement) from that class was taken in Round 17 (and yes, he's in the book). Justin Verlander tops the 2004 Draft WAR list, but fourth on that list is another 17th-rounder (also in the book). You'll also find a 13th-round selection headed to the Hall of Fame in this book; a fifth-rounder who leads his draft class in WAR, has an MVP Award, and two World Series rings; a ninth-round pick who used to be a shortstop and has gone on to win two Cy Young Awards; a soft-tossing college performer taken in the fourth round who leads his class in WAR (through the 2022 season) and has a Cy Young Award on his shelf; and two surprise second-round picks, one a Canadian high schooler who is second among all 2002 draftees in WAR, the other a college senior who didn't hit until his final year at that level and has gone on to win a batting title and two Silver Slugger Awards.

There are more success stories than could possibly fit into one book (sequel, anyone?). The moral of the story? Pay attention to the draft beyond the first round. And if you meet a scout? Thank him for all he's done to ensure the continuation of our national pastime.

Chapter 1

Joey Votto

Kasey McKeon and John Castleberry knew they were onto something, and they knew they had to keep it quiet. Scouts, as an occupational hazard, often keep things close to the vest, and many in the industry could qualify for jobs with the CIA because of their ability to stay tight-lipped when it comes to opinions on players. So McKeon, the scouting director, and Castleberry, the special assignment scout, knew how to keep a secret.

It was 2002, a time when scouting subterfuge was tougher to maintain due to the proliferation of travel ball and showcase events. But the Cincinnati Reds scouting duo of McKeon and Castleberry, along with a very tight inner circle, wanted to keep their interest in a young high school hitter from Ontario, Canada, on the down low. This wasn't only to keep other teams off the scent of Joey Votto. There was a traitor in their midst and, as a result, a need to keep other members of the Reds front office in the dark.

It would help land Cincinnati one of the best hitters of his generation, one who has gone from being a second-round selection in 2002 to a career Red, who's won a National League

Most Valuable Player Award and has been named to a half-dozen All-Star teams through 2022.

And it would ultimately lead to the pair losing their jobs.

————

It's better to be lucky than good. That well-worn axiom could be the tagline for just about any scout in baseball. And Kasey McKeon was certainly lucky to have stumbled on Joey Votto in the fall of 2001.

McKeon is the son of baseball lifer Jack McKeon, who won a World Series as the Marlins manager in 2003 and earned the moniker "Trader Jack" when he was general manager of the Padres in the 1980s. After a brief minor league career, Kasey McKeon entered the world of scouting, first working for the Padres, then moving to the Indians and then to the Reds, who hired him as a major league scout and a national crosschecker after the 1998 season. He ascended to the scouting director chair in the late summer of 2000, so when he arrived in Jupiter, Florida, the Spring Training home of the Cardinals and Marlins and the site for the Perfect Game World Wood Bat Association (WWBA) World Championship, he had one draft in charge under his belt.

Ask anyone who has ever attended Perfect Game's WWBA World Championship and they'll tell you it's both a very valuable stop to see a ton of talent in one place and an absolute zoo. Dozens of teams, hundreds of players, often 50 or more games a day. Scouts descend on Jupiter every fall for this event. They are long, grueling days, but it's usually the last chance to see high school talent before the following spring. Usually held in October, it's thought of as the unofficial end of the big showcase season.

The McKeon baseball family extends far and wide. Kasey's brother-in-law was Greg Booker, the former big league pitcher and scout (while general manager with the Padres, Jack McKeon traded his son-in-law to the Minnesota Twins, which must have made for a fun Thanksgiving family gathering that fall). Games start very early in the morning at the WWBA event, as early as 8:00 AM.

And the 2001 version of the event was packed with talent, with B.J. Upton, Zack Grienke, and Prince Fielder, all top 10 picks in the 2002 Draft, on hand. But Kasey McKeon was out early because he wanted to check in on his nephew, Zach Booker, Greg's son, who would eventually go on to play for Elon University and spend a few years in the lower levels of the minor leagues and is now a college coach.

Booker had been picked up to play in the tournament by a North Carolina team and that morning, they would be facing a team sponsored by *Baseball America*, a squad that featured eventual 2003 No. 1 overall pick Delmon Young and had a third baseman from Toronto: Joey Votto.

"As scouts do, I think, you pay attention," McKeon said. "So I'm watching this kid at third base and it's like wow, this is a good-sized kid, swings the bat, good approach. So that was the start of it."

McKeon's interest was piqued after a brief exchange with Votto after that morning game about Canada's national pastime. Seeing that Votto was from Toronto, McKeon asked a simple question.

"Who's your favorite hockey team?"

"I don't really care about hockey," is how McKeon remembers Votto responding.

"I thought, 'Wow, you don't meet many Canadians who don't like hockey or don't really care for hockey.' And I just kind of logged that info."

Some might have seen that response as a reason to rescind Votto's citizenship, but McKeon saw it as a sign that this kid with a smooth left-handed swing was clearly serious about baseball.

Paul Pierson, now the Reds' amateur scouting assistant director, was a baseball operations assistant who handled logistics for
the scouting department as well as going out and seeing players.
He remembers McKeon getting locked in on Votto's swing almost
immediately.

"I do remember sitting with Kasey one game and just watching Joey swinging the bat," Pierson said. "And Kasey was getting
pretty excited about what he saw from a scouting perspective,
from the love of his swing to his plate discipline, even at a younger
age, just his overall feel to hit. I think Kasey took notice and it
really started from there.

"That was kind of his gut feel. You know, we always give our
area guys a 'Who was your gut feel going into the year?' guy.
That was Kasey's gut feel guy."

McKeon wanted to make sure it wasn't just his gut. So he
beckoned John Castleberry to come with him to check out Votto
in his next game.

Castleberry was relatively new to the Reds but was no stranger
to scouting and baseball. A former college coach, he was one
of the first scouts hired by the then-Florida Marlins, working
for legendary scouting director Gary Hughes. Hughes left the
Marlins for the Rockies in 1999 then moved on to the Reds in
2000. Hughes worked with McKeon to create a hybrid position for Castleberry that included professional scouting as well
as crosschecking on the amateur side. The gig included handling
Canada because the Reds didn't have a dedicated scout north of
the border, so if anyone was going to check out Votto, it was
going to be Castleberry.

"He calls me up and tells me he needs me right away," said
Castleberry, recalling that Votto was playing on one of the very
back fields at the time. "So I scramble, I jog down there as best
as I can and I get down to the field and he says, 'I want you to
watch this guy.'"

"I want you to go see this kid because I've got a feeling I'm going to draft him," McKeon said he told Castleberry.

Castleberry then proceeds to see Votto absolutely smoke a ball into right field, showing off the swing, the timing, the balance that got McKeon so excited.

"I think, 'Holy crap, who is this guy?'" said Castleberry, who is now a crosschecker for the San Francisco Giants. He couldn't wait to see more.

Except McKeon wouldn't let him. After the single-swing confirmation, he wants him and Castleberry to clear out, lest anyone else see that two high-level scouts from the Reds are sitting on one, relatively unknown hitter. Castleberry tried to put up a fight, to no avail.

"I've got Canada and this guy's a Canadian, I should probably stay," Castleberry told McKeon. "Kasey thinks like an old-time scout and says, 'I don't want to give anybody notice that we're watching this kid.' So we just walked away. I said, 'Dude, I have to see this guy play.' He says, 'Don't worry about it, we'll figure it out.' So that was my view of Joey Votto. It was a good one-swing look, but it's still one swing."

———

Joey Votto wasn't a complete unknown at this point, but it was close. He had participated in Perfect Game's National Showcase earlier in the summer, but that had been about it. This isn't one of those instances, however, where a young player is salty about not being seen, or felt he was unappreciated. In fact, there's a lot of understanding, a forgiveness from the "slighted" party.

"To be fair to any scouts in the area, I wasn't a really standout prospect," Votto said. "I didn't run the 60 well, I didn't throw hard relative to a lot of the interesting starting pitching prospects, I was a corner infielder at best, and I didn't have ridiculous power that you just had to come see. So I was not the type of prospect that I think the average scout would be interested in following just because there wasn't much that really stood out about me. And so I did not get a lot of interest."

There were some other variables that certainly contributed to Votto not being on most radar screens by the fall of 2001. The first was geography. It's not that there hadn't been, or continues to be, good talent coming from Canada. There are two Hall of Famers, after all, in right-handed pitcher Fergie Jenkins and outfielder Larry Walker, but both entered pro ball before Canada was added to the draft in 1991. Walker is from British Columbia, all the way on the western side of the country, and while Jenkins is from Ontario, he began his pro career before the draft era started in 1965.

Votto is from Toronto and a majority of the successful players from Canada have come from elsewhere. Russell Martin is from Quebec and was drafted late by the Montreal Expos out of high school in 2000, but didn't get started until two years later when the Dodgers drafted him out of Chipola Junior College in Florida. Through the 2022 season, there have been a grand total of 17 players, including Votto, from Ontario to make it at all to the big leagues. And Votto is one of just eight who had recorded a positive career WAR through the 2022 season.

"To be honest with you, Toronto hasn't really had a big prospect maybe in ever," Votto said. "I'm talking about a Byron Buxton or a Gerrit Cole, a very clear No. 1 pick or a top five pick. I don't ever remember going to a game where there were more than a few scouts."

Added to the mix was that Votto was in 13th grade at the time. Yes, that's a thing. In Ontario, students are required to spend five years in high school. The technical name for that fifth year is called Ontario Academic Credit (OAC), though everyone just calls it Grade 13. There were two sides of that coin for Votto.

On the plus side, it gave him an extra year to mature. On the flip side, it didn't fit in the normal rhythm of when high school players are scouted and drafted.

The age of a player when drafted has always been taken into consideration and might even carry more weight now than it did when Votto was coming out. Teams have computer models that consider all different variables, and age is big one. If a high school player is deemed too old for his class, some teams' models will reject that player. A recent example of that is with Mets 2019 first-round pick Brett Baty. Baty was considered one of the best pure hitters of that draft class, but because he was 19 on draft day, some teams wouldn't even consider him, with the thought process being that an older player would dominate high school competition more regularly. Needless to say, Baty hit his way to Double-A in 2021, where he was nearly three years younger than the average hitter in his league, and made his big league debut a year later. While those models didn't exist at the turn of the 21st century, there's no question age was important. Working in Votto's favor is that he would have still been 17 had he come out in the 2001 Draft and with a September birthday, would have just turned 18 when McKeon and the Reds saw him in Jupiter.

"I probably didn't really round myself out as a player until that 13th year, until that fifth year of high school," Votto admitted. "And so when high school players, my competitors, were preparing for American college, I was going into, preparing for my final year of high school."

It was during the fall of that final year that Votto found himself in Jupiter player in the WWBA event that allowed McKeon to lay eyes on him for the first time. Some players come to showcases like that knowing they belong in conversations about the first couple of rounds of the Draft and are using an event like that to boost their stock. Then there are players like Votto. Like any young player, he dreamed of continuing his career, and had committed to Coastal Carolina, a smaller Division I school that has produced a fair amount of professional talent over the years. Competing in Jupiter, however, gave the future All-Star a sense of exactly where he stood among his peers.

"I thought it was an opportunity... as someone that came from a very modest league, I didn't know how good I was. The idea of playing professionally was kind of far-fetched coming from where I came from, and I just wanted to see if I was good enough. And it turns out I played relatively well.

"And more than anything, it boosted my confidence and told me, 'Holy cow, maybe you have a chance to be reasonable.' And, you know, I got to play with Delmon Young and he was the first overall pick. And I thought, 'Holy cow, if I can play with him, maybe I have a chance here.'

"I didn't have confidence. Confidence is only as good as what you can do, your experiences. And I was not at all feeling like I was an intriguing prospect. I was motivated, and I wanted to be good. But I had no idea whether or not I had any sort of chance at all. To be fair, I also still thought at the same time I was going to make it and I thought I was going to be a good player, just because I was motivated."

––––––––––

Votto's motivation paired nicely with learning the nuances of the game from Bob Smyth. Smyth is a Canadian coaching legend who was also an associate scout with the Seattle Mariners who ran what served as the local baseball academy. He coached Votto at Richview Collegiate and also with the Ebticoke Rangers. Votto once told the *Toronto Star* that Smyth "was and is the most important baseball person I've ever had in my life. My dad introduced me to baseball, and he certainly was right there, head-to-head, in terms of his impact."

"If you told him to work on something, he'd go and do it," Smyth told MacLeans. For Votto, it was a match made in baseball heaven.

"I was very fortunate to be able to work with him, the ins and outs," he said. "He helped shape my career in such a way that I think matched up with professional baseball."

Anyone who has seen Votto on a major league field, in the batting cage, knows what a tireless worker he is. You need to seek perfection to be a successful big league hitter, even if the best in the business fail two-thirds of the time. (Votto had a career .297 average through the 2022 season, so even he failed 70 percent of the time.)

There's one story from Votto's high school days, from that final year, that epitomizes who Votto was and who he would become. Naeem Saddiq learned from Smyth and coached in the area as well, actually coaching Richview before Votto got there and seeing him at Etobicoke.

"He wasn't that kid who was a phenom kid at a young age that everyone thought was going to make it," said Saddiq, who now works for the Ontario Principals Council, an association for principals and vice principals at schools around the province. "He was a solid player who just got better year after year.

"The kids I see now who are highly touted, they have an air about them. And sometimes there's an arrogance or a reluctance to interact with other kids or people. Joey wasn't like that. The one thing Joey would constantly do is ask everyone for advice, he'd ask everyone for input. He was grounded by what Bob would tell him to do, and Bob was sort of the filter."

Saddiq was on the receiving end of that ask more than once, but there is one instance that now does seem like "quintessential Votto," when Saddiq, now coaching at Etobicoke Collegiate, the rival of Votto's Richview. The two teams would always meet in the finals, and in 2002, most felt Richview would win because of

Votto. Saddiq, to his credit, told his pitchers during the regular season to pitch to him because he could tell at that point Votto had a chance to play at the next level and didn't want to take the bat out of his hands.

During the regular season matchup at Etobicoke's field, Saddiq had his best lefty, Travis Gilligan, on the mound. Gilligan was as quality a high school pitcher the region had, a southpaw who could get the ball up into the upper-80s with some good secondary stuff. And Saddiq told Gilligan to go after Votto, who proceeded to put a ball on the roof of the community center across the way, one on the street.

Gilligan asked Saddiq when Votto came up for the last time if there was any way to get him out. Saddiq's advice was to start with some off-speed stuff to get Votto to pull the ball a mile foul, then maybe there'd be a chance of getting Votto lunging a bit on his front foot. Sure enough, Gilligan executed the plan and got Votto to pop out.

Any typical high school player would have been content with the handful of hits, home runs, and runs batted in Votto collected that day. Votto, clearly, was anything but typical. Saddiq can't help but smile when retelling what transpired next:

"So the game's over, we shake hands. He's standing behind me. 'Hey Coach, how's it going? How'd I do today?' I was like, 'You did well, you lost three of my baseballs.' He said, 'How'd you get me out?' Because he could see I was talking to Travis. And I said, 'Well, he got you on your front foot. You're trying to swing hard and you got a little ahead of yourself.'"

Saddiq knew that Votto had already worked with Smyth and Smyth's mentor Nick Rico on this. They preached an approach, staying spread out in the box to avoid lunging, and it would be something Votto could lean on to avoid doing so in the future. But Saddiq didn't quite know who he was dealing with and that Votto would want to work on it, right then and there.

"So I go back to school, put away the stuff, drive a couple of kids home and now I'm coming back past the park on the way home and there he is, with his friend Warren Bradley, hitting balls. I asked, 'What are you doing?' He says, 'Oh, I have to work on staying off my front foot.'"

Of course, the two schools met in the final, as predicted. For a championship, Etobicoke didn't pitch to Votto.

"We're not stupid, right?" Saddiq joked.

That is, until the end of the game, when Etobicoke was up 8–0 and Votto comes up for one last at-bat.

"Travis kind of looks at me," Saddiq said about his left-handed ace who pitched the title game as well. "So I go up to the mound and he says, 'I think I want to try to get him out.' It's 8–0, so I say, 'Well, you've earned the chance.' I don't think I sat down before the ball was gone. And I think that's Joey's last amateur swing."

As the spring season leading into the 2002 Draft got started, the Reds didn't know too much about this piece, the makeup and work ethic that helped Joey Votto go from "not so intriguing prospect" to potential Hall of Famer. And they knew they needed to see more of him, no matter how convinced McKeon was that he wanted to draft him based on one tournament. But they needed to do it under a shroud of secrecy.

As an assistant to McKeon, Pierson was tasked with finding out when and where Votto would be playing. Making it more challenging was that McKeon wanted few others, both outside and inside the organization, to know about their interest.

"I used writer Bob Elliott as a tremendous resource for what they were doing," Pierson said. "I primarily used him and some websites in finding out where these guys were playing. And Kasey had me do a little bit of the groundwork behind the scenes and told me keep everything hush hush. In the springtime, I don't remember a lot of people going up there on purpose because Kasey did not want anyone to even know he was on him. We can't tell anyone, because we're worried about that information getting out."

Scouting directors often don't want to tip their hand to other clubs, especially when there's a player that's relatively obscured from view. The spring of 2002 was probably right at the end of an era when such a thing was possible. It's not that talent emerges "out of nowhere" now, but the explosion of showcases and travel ball have made it increasingly harder to hide a player. The Reds tried to do just that, though Castleberry made sure to see him more than once.

The first time came via a workout put on by the Major League Baseball Scouting Bureau. The MLSB was an invaluable resource for teams, especially in Canada, when it wasn't always so easy to time trips to see players or get the weather to cooperate. And the 2002 Draft class was a rich one in terms of Canadian talent, so Castleberry had to see several players that spring, not just Votto, and not just in the Toronto area.

The Reds picked No. 3 overall that year and one of the players in the mix was Adam Loewen, a talented two-way high school player from British Columbia (a western province for those unfamiliar with Canadian geography), who would end up going one pick after the Reds took California prep right-hander Chris Gruler to the Orioles as a left-handed pitcher. The University of British Columbia also had a talented lefty in Jeff Francis, who ended up as the No. 7 overall pick, taken by the Rockies. Shawn Bowman was a high school infielder from BC the Mets drafted and signed in Round 12 and Scott Mathieson eventually made it to the big leagues after the Phillies took him in the 17th round.

Back east, the Ontario amateur baseball scene was also home to Chris Leroux, then a high school catcher the Rays would take in the ninth round. He didn't sign, went on to Winthrop University in South Carolina, converted to the mound and eventually made it to the big leagues as a reliever.

"It was kind of a perfect storm in Canada at that time," said Walt Burrows, who was then was Major League Scouting Bureau's Canada director and now scouts the nation for the Minnesota Twins. "The 2002 Draft class was the class of all classes in Canada, with Adam Loewen, who to this day is the best high school player I've ever seen in Canada, and Jeff Francis. There were two first rounders there that everybody knew about. And there were other players there, with Joey being one of them."

All of this is to say Castleberry had his hands full covering Canada while attending to all of his other jack-of-all-trades duties with the Reds that year. So he was thrilled whenever the Scouting Bureau had an event he could attend. He went to one out west to see Loewen and was able to arrange his travel to head to Toronto for a workout put on by Burrows. It was early May and it was supposed to take place at Bob Smyth's field. But since this was eastern Canada in early spring, it of course rained, meaning Castleberry's first look at Votto after the one swing in Jupiter was indoors, in a hitting cage.

It might be kind to call the indoor area where Burrows put the Canadian players through their paces a "facility." Perhaps it was bigger than a bread box, but not by much. Burrows recalled that it had to be around 60 feet wide because they had a mound for pitching workouts. But if it was 60 × 40, it was a lot. Since he was new to the territory, Castleberry could still try to follow the script of being somewhat incognito despite the size of the place.

"Nobody really knew who I was, just that I worked with Cincinnati." Castleberry said. "And I'm standing in the back. He's hitting two cages down. And he is taking the net off with his swings. I had never seen such violence in the swing. It was impressive. It was coming off his bat, they didn't have exit speed back then, but if they did, even in the cage… I literally put my hand over my mouth and just went, 'Oh my God, this guy's gonna kill [someone], it's going to go through the net.'"

"The cage was maybe about 30 feet long," Burrows said. "There was kind of like an L screen and then there was a hanging net at the back to stop balls being hit. Joey hit all these balls and they just barely go over the L screen, hit this net behind and ricochet back to the guy that was throwing BP to the point that he had to put helmet on."

Castleberry stayed until the very end of the workout, he asked Burrows if Votto could take more swings and Burrows recalls Votto taking 100 more swings after the place had basically cleared out. Castleberry was hoping to get some one-on-one face time with Votto when no one would be any the wiser, though there was one other scout, Jim Chapman with the Dodgers, who also waited him out, so it was a tag-team interview in the end.

"I'm thinking, 'God this sucks.' I really wanted to spend time with him just myself," Castleberry said. "But we sat down and talked to Joey and peppered him with questions. I got to know him a little bit. Impressive kid, for a guy his age, he really understood the game, you could tell he was very mature."

After the workout, Castleberry reached out to McKeon to report in, telling his boss that while he only saw him indoors, McKeon's instincts seemed to be spot on. Where Votto was going to play defensively remained in question—he certainly wasn't going to play shortstop like he did at times for his high school, and likely wasn't a third baseman or an outfielder. Some, including Castleberry, thought he could catch, and he worked out there some—but the indoor workout helped confirm what McKeon thought he saw: That bat had the chance to be special.

———————

Unbeknownst to the Reds, they were not the only ones who liked Votto dating back from the WWBA tournament in Florida, and it wasn't the Dodgers who were really vying for him. The New York Yankees, right at the end of a run that saw them win four World Series and appear in five over a six-year period, had also fallen in love with Votto's swing. Unlike the Reds, who tried to keep their interest hidden, Yankee scout Fernando Arango wanted to make sure the young Canadian hitter saw him for each and every at-bat in Jupiter, that's how excited he was. And Arango was sure to relay just how good he thought Votto was to legendary Yankees scout Dick Groch.

At the time, Groch was the team's scout in the Midwest, handling Ohio, Michigan, parts of Indiana, maybe dipping into Illinois. While Groch has signed more players than could be counted, the one most wanted to know about was a skinny high school shortstop from Michigan he helped convince the Yankees to take in the first round 10 years earlier, in 1992. That, of course, was Derek Jeter, the Hall of Famer who is synonymous with the Yankees dynasty doing all that winning when Votto's year came around.

As part of his responsibilities, Groch also was the Yankees' presence in Canada, and had been dating back to before the draft era. Groch loved scouting Canada, perhaps because of the challenges it presented at the time in terms of finding talent and dealing with the adverse weather conditions. And he valued his Yankees colleague's opinion. Arango, who later would try to bang the table for a junior college infielder named Albert Pujols while serving as a scout for the Rays, really liked Votto, so Groch made sure he found time to see him.

Working in conjunction with an associate scout, Richie Clemens, Groch made sure he got Votto's schedule and Clemens attended every game Votto played for his high school in that 13th grade season for Richview Collegiate Institute. It was hard to see Votto otherwise. While not poor, Votto's parents had relatively modest means and paying for regular travel ball wasn't possible. Current Yankees scouting director Damon Oppenheimer remembers going to cross-check Votto that spring, throwing batting practice in a public park and using a metal trash can as an L screen for protection, then went to watch him play in a men's league game that night. Not exactly you're typical scouting venues.

Groch himself went and saw Votto play in a doubleheader early in the spring and saw enough there to confirm his interest. And when he worked him out after those two games, he had his own unusual BP story to tell, relating an exchange he had with Votto when he came to the plate and Groch was ready to throw from a typical spot for BP, in front of the mound. The conversation, according to Groch, went something like this:

> Votto: I don't think you should do that from there.
> Groch: Why is that, Joey?
> Votto: Well, my dad never does.
> Groch: Why not?
> Votto: See the 401 Highway?
> Groch: Yeah
> Votto: Well, I hit them into the highway and my dad's concerned I'm going to cause an accident.

"I'm looking at the 401 and I'm thinking to get there, my God, I'm going to have to rent a car. So I say, 'Well, Joey, let's try it. Three balls, two in the highway'. I say, 'That's enough.' So what I had to do is position myself between in front of the third base dugout, right in the middle, facing the mound. He's hitting left-handed from the front of the dugout. And two of the 10 balls that I throw did make it out. And I said, 'We have to find another field to hit in.' The hitting was there, the power was there."

––––––––

While all this was going on, Castleberry was pestering McKeon about seeing Votto in actual action. And he wanted to be sure others in the department got to see him as well. Figuring out how to orchestrate that without many folks knowing was easier said than done. And the window to see Votto in game action was a small one, considering the season doesn't start in Ontario until early May and the draft is a month later.

After waiting for as long as possible, McKeon hatched a plan to bring in a group of trusted scouts to see Votto en masse. The Reds scouting director was going to be in Bowling Green, Ohio, for the Middle Atlantic Conference (MAC) Tournament and had Billy Scherrer, then the Reds' East Coast cross-checker and now a special assistant to White Sox GM Rick Hahn, and Johnny Almaraz, then the assistant scouting director and now a pro scout for the Marlins. McKeon also had brought in the late Jeff Barton from the West Coast. Picking at No. 3, they all went to the MAC tourney to watch Ball State ace Bryan Bullington, who would end up going No. 1 overall to the Pirates.

But that was only step one in the plan. The Bullington game was at 10:00 AM and after its completion the quartet of Reds scouts sped to the airport in Detroit to fly to Toronto. There, Castleberry was waiting with a van to take them to finally see Votto in action. It's pretty tough to stay incognito when you show up to a game in Ontario, pour out of a van and stream into a ballpark five deep. But that didn't stop the Reds from trying to play it cool, with this Fab Five heading off in different directions upon entering the ballpark as if that would somehow throw off the scent.

"We devise this plan that now really kind of looks stupid in the long run, but it was like, 'Okay, you go this way, I'm gonna go this way; we can't tip our hand, we don't know who's there,'" McKeon said. "We don't know what other scouts are there and that's what we did. Billy Scherrer went one way, Almaraz and I went another way, Castleberry went the other way."

Castleberry and Barton noticed the starting pitcher that day seemed to have a good delivery and arm action when they saw him warming up in the bullpen. And it was Barton who suggested breaking out the radar gun to create the ruse they were there to scout the starting pitcher that day, all while watching Votto's every move out of the corner of their eyes.

"He topped out at like 78 mph," Castleberry said. "We just started laughing."

"We watch him warm up, he steps on the mound and Billy's like, 'Well, there goes that,'" McKeon recalled. "Okay, this charade is over. Let's just go focus on Joey and the heck with it. We've got two, maybe three weeks before the draft, so I don't believe anybody can get in here and upstage us."

There were two other scouts at that game, according to Castleberry. One was Canadian scouting legend Jim Ridley, then with the Blue Jays. The other was a young scout with the Yankees, Clemens. Castleberry remembers Ridley on the phone all game, guessing he was taken aback by the Reds' shock and awe.

Votto didn't set the world on fire that day, no one really remembers what his stat line was, but it certainly didn't detract from anyone's desire to draft him. Castleberry chauffeured everyone back across the border, with a stop for Canadian beer and a look at Niagara Falls on the way, before returning the van and getting back on the road to cover the rest of the SEC tournament.

Ridley's appearance at that game begs the question: Were the Blue Jays on their hometown kid? The answer, in a word, is... no. That might surprise some who watch the draft landscape each year nowadays, when the Blue Jays try to make sure they don't let other teams beat them in terms of drafting local talent.

Aside from Votto having generally flown under the radar, not playing for the big travel team or for the junior national team, he was one thing the Blue Jays of that era avoided as much as Superman steers clear of kryptonite: a high school player.

In November of the previous season, the Blue Jays had hired J.P. Ricciardi to be the general manager. Early in 2002, he brought Keith Law, who had gained some prominence as an analytics-minded writer for Baseball Prospectus, on board to help build the organization's philosophy. And while it's overly simplistic to boil it down to just this, the nutshell version was: draft college players. Keep in mind, this year would turn out to be the "Moneyball" draft, made famous by Michael Lewis' deep dive into how Billy Beane and the Oakland A's used data and analytics much more to make decisions, and in 2002, that meant drafting college players with more of that data to consider.

In 2002, 13 of the Jays' top 15 picks were all college players, starting with North Carolina infielder Russ Adams in the first round. Votto wasn't going to be on their board under any circumstance, so he really wasn't scouted. The Blue Jays didn't track him down in Jupiter when McKeon stumbled on him. They didn't really watch him at all in the spring, until his name started bubbling up toward the surface a bit more.

"With Joey, he was one of those kids who kind of slid through the cracks up here because he didn't play anywhere," said Bill Byckowski, who was then a cross-checker for the Blue Jays and is now, ironically, in a similar role with the Reds. "It was just by chance the Reds saw him. We didn't know him.

"He was basically in a beer league and nobody saw this guy play. He goes down [to Florida] and hits the ball hard and he comes back and nobody knows who he is. We knew every kid in Canada; if the guy can play, we knew everything about a kid. But remember, he wasn't drafted in 12th grade and had zero exposure. We used to know all the bad players, let alone the good players. To not have Joey Votto on the list somewhere would have been impossible. But because of the circumstances, we didn't."

"The circumstances" was the college focus of that year's draft for Toronto. But even with that, they did eventually catch wind of Votto. Byckowski was at the SEC Tournament when he got a call from Ridley, urging the cross-checker to check out the young Canadian hitter, perhaps pushed to do so while seeing the Reds arrive en masse.

Listening to his veteran scout, Byckowski did due diligence and went to see Votto play, only to witness a brutal 0-for-4 night against a soft-tossing lefty.

"He's playing in a high school game, and he's catching, and he's not a very good catcher," Byckowski recalled. "I get two strikeouts, a pop up, and a 17-hopper. I can't write this guy up; I don't know what to make of this."

It wasn't the last the cross-checker heard about Votto, however. Mark Snipp was a national scout for Toronto that year and he called Byckowski up about Votto, hearing buzz that he was going to get drafted pretty high. So they brought him in for a workout at the SkyDome. Byckowski got reports that he put a few balls into the upper deck, but it was too little, too late.

"We didn't have history on the kid," Byckowski said. "We weren't taking high school kids from anywhere. I don't think we would've taken him under any circumstances."

———

Those workouts in a home stadium can mean a lot to teams, sometimes too much. A player can come in right before the draft and a good or weak performance can shift the decision-makers' opinions within an organization one way or the other. Recency bias is very real and can swing the pendulum in either direction.

For the Reds scouts who were on the Votto train, there was much more at stake than just Votto's performance when they arranged to get him to come to what was then known as Cinergy Field (the old Riverfront Stadium) for a workout. This was going to be the time when the proverbial cat would be out of the bag. After spending much of the spring keeping Votto hidden, he would no longer be a secret after taking some swings on the big-league field.

The first challenge was getting him there. While much of the industry was still sleeping on the Canadian, he had performed well enough, often enough, at things like Scouting Bureau workouts, to earn a few invitations to work out for teams. Castleberry caught wind that Votto was heading to Los Angeles for one and because he remembered Jim Chapman being with him at that indoor workout, he assumed it was the Dodgers. When talking to the Vottos, he found out it was the Angels, giving the Reds scout another team to worry about.

With days dwindling before the draft and other workouts planned, figuring out the logistics were tough. Then a light went off in Castleberry's head when he was informed that Votto was planning on going to Columbus, then the Triple-A affiliate for the Yankees, to work out. He had a plan to get Votto to Cincinnati and save the cash-strapped organization some money.

"Cincinnati was known for its workouts. We brought in Scott Kazmir, because we're picking three, and we brought in the guy we took, Gruler," Castleberry said, adding that others in the department wanted to see if it would be possible to get Votto in as well since they knew McKeon was eyeing him fairly early.

"In order for me to be able to get him taken or to take him, I needed the big boys at least to see him," McKeon said. "[General manager] Jim Bowden needed to see him and lay eyes on him and I had to hope for the best."

After talking with the Vottos, it was clear there was a window the day before the workout in Columbus that could work.

"He can fly into Cincinnati on the Yankees' dime. We'll pick him up when he gets there, we'll put him up for the night and then they can pick him up at the stadium," Castleberry recounts with a chuckle. And on the tail end, the Reds made the Yankees scout wait an extra two hours in his car outside of the ballpark as they took their time with Votto after his workout.

"The Yankees can always wait a little longer," Castleberry quipped.

What happened between Votto's arrival in Cincy and his delayed departure to Columbus is the stuff legends are made of; the kind of performance scouts talk about in hushed tones. Castleberry recalls Votto crushing the ball all over the field, including some upper-deck shots. And he did it against some high-end arms, from draft prospects to minor league free agents looking for jobs. And he caught, too, all these arms, throwing much harder than anything Votto had seen regularly in Toronto. Votto, never one to shy away from an opportunity to be self-effacing, believes what evaluators that day thought was a glimpse at the outstanding approach he's shown throughout his career, was more about him not seeing the 90-plus heat than him spitting on it because it was off the plate.

"It was all just too fast; I was trying to catch up with it," Votto said. "And I looked like I was checking off. And I still do that same sort of shit to this day when I'm over-matched. I hit a changeup for a home run. It wasn't a good fastball that I hit, I hit a changeup. And they were like, 'Whoa, okay, he's got some power and he can hit.' And it was just me trying to time the fastball and hitting their change."

And he did it in front of scouts, the general manager and Reds greats like Hall of Famer Johnny Bench and future Hall of Famer Ken Griffey Jr., who was on the disabled list during his third season with Cincinnati at the time. Votto impressed many with his knowledge of Bench and how respectful he was around him, while giving some a heart attack when he decided to imitate Junior Griffey's bat waggle while taking batting practice.

"Ken Griffey Jr. was the ultimate for me at the time," Votto said. "And he was there. And I just thought it was fun. I have a little bit of a playful streak in me. I got called out in the middle of that little thing where I tried to imitate Junior and I rolled over a couple balls. And they said, 'He doesn't do that.' And I thought it was funny. And I just kept hitting. I was just having fun."

"He looks over at Junior," Castleberry said, "and says, 'Hey, Junior, who's this?' And he imitates Junior and I'm saying, 'Oh, Jesus Christ, Joseph, what are you doing?'"

Poor mimicry aside, what Votto was doing was making a very strong impression. And that was in front of some important people who, until that point, didn't know he existed.

"His BP was really good. He really drove the ball," Pierson said. "It was kind of a little bit of an 'Oh shit' moment because all of the special assistants and all of Jim's guys were there. And at that point in time, I think they started to realize, 'Who is this guy? Who got him here? We should have had a ton of people see this guy.' And I think it really started to snowball from there."

In any good spy thriller, it's important not to reveal the secret until the end of the story, or at least close to it. McKeon and his scouts kept Votto under wraps for as long as they could, not just to keep other teams off the scent, but because of a perceived mole within the organization.

Jim Bowden had been the general manager of the Reds since October 1992 and had built a team of senior advisors that included veteran baseball men like Larry Barton, Gene Bennett, Bob Boone (who was manager of the Reds at the time), Al Goldis, Gary Hughes and his top advisor, Leland Maddox. He felt having that inner circle essential, based on lessons he had learned in watching others do business.

Bowden tells the story of the 1992 Draft, when he was the director of player development for the Reds, so he was in the draft room when conversations were happening, though not part of the decision-making apparatus. But he sat there with scouts like Barton and Bennett, who were trying to convince then-scouting director Julian Mock to go check out a high school shortstop one more time. But Mock was set on taking toolsy college outfielder Chad Mottola and could not be persuaded to head to Michigan to check out the infielder Barton and Bennett wanted. The Reds took Mottola, who did touch the big leagues for four different teams in five different seasons, with the fifth pick. The Yankees had the next pick and, thanks to the efforts of Dick Groch—yes, the same Dick Groch who would be the Reds' main competition for Votto—selected the shortstop Barton and Bennett wanted: Hall of Famer Derek Jeter.

That provides some context as to why Bowden was upset that his senior advisors weren't clued into Votto and why he was so surprised that day at Cinergy Field.

"I remember looking over and going, 'Who the hell is that?'" said Bowden, who is now a baseball analyst on SiriusXM Satellite radio and writes for The Athletic after serving as GM for the Washington Nationals following his tenure in Cincinnati. "It was one of those bats that just stood out. The swing, the confidence, the whole thing. It's one of those bats that when you see it, you just know he's going to hit. I said, 'Where's this guy been?'"

Bowden posed that question to his senior advisors, who told him that no one had asked them to go see Votto prior to this workout. Bowden responded with incredulity, "What do you mean you didn't see him? How can this kid be here and we didn't see him?"

The how and why is that there was fear of an internal leak. Many of the Bowden's inner circle were extremely well-respected, but not all close to the GM were trusted. Information about players had a tendency to get out to other clubs, with deep suspicion of a strong Reds top advisor-to-Milwaukee Brewers information pipeline occurring, for example.

"We had a couple of guys who were a little, I don't know how to word it right, sleazy or snaky," Castleberry said. "So we found we had a mole in our group and every time we would mention a player, the guy that he was tight with worked for Milwaukee, then Milwaukee was on the same players, just out of the blue. And we figured out who this was, so during this whole process, I would never mention a word about Joey."

Bowden, for his part, feels that if McKeon and others had that concern, they needed to take it to a superior, namely him, and let him know. But it's a Catch-22 if the main area of worry stemmed from someone that superior trusted the most. So they kept it quiet and dealt with the consequences: Castleberry was fired in July and McKeon's contract was not renewed. Now, years later, Bowden does have to give credit where credit is due.

"I went through more scouting directors than George Steinbrenner did managers because we just didn't get it right, to be honest with you," Bowden said. "When Kasey came in, I thought he had good judgment. I thought he would listen to the older evaluators to get everyone's opinions. Instead, he and John Castleberry, Bill Scherrer... he did trust Johnny Almaraz, which is a good thing because he was one of our better evaluators back then. So they kept it from our expensive guys and my whole fear was I didn't want another Jeter thing to happen, so that was a process problem.

"At the end of the day, the bottom line is this: Great scouting by Kasey McKeon, great cross-checking by Castleberry, Scherrer, and Almaraz, they got this 17-year-old player out of nowhere, they brought him into our house, we took him and he's going to the Hall of Fame. And it's a great story and those guys deserve all the credit. As a GM, did I like the process? Not really. But it's a result-oriented business and they got the job done."

―――――

Liking a player or wanting to draft him and actually getting a player are not often the same thing, and volumes could be filled with stories of "players we liked that someone else took." So just because Votto had impressed during the workout a few days before the draft, just because McKeon had him targeted for a certain area, did not make this a slam dunk. There were other teams interested, namely the Yankees, and there were financial considerations to weigh.

That year, the Reds scouting department had been shorted about $1 million, with money moved from the domestic amateur scouting department to help pay for an international signee. In 2002, there were no signing bonus pools or penalties for going over a certain spending amount. Teams could, if they wanted to, spend as much as they wanted to on any given player and in any given draft. But the Reds, for the most part, were not the kind of franchise to spend wildly in this market.

As a result, decisions had to be made, some of them on the fly as the draft unfolded. Many in the scouting department wanted to take Scott Kazmir, the high school lefty, with that pick at No. 3 overall. But his price tag was thought to be higher, and given that No. 1 pick Bryan Bullington signed for an under-slot $4 million, No. 2 pick B.J. Upton signed for $4.6 million, and No. 4 pick Adam Loewen ended up singing a major league deal worth just north of $4 million, it's easy to guesstimate Kazmir's asking price could have easily been in that range as well. The Reds would never find out and, in the end, they went the high school right-hander route and took Chris Gruler, who would sign for a below-slot $2.5 million, still a franchise record at the time.

The Reds had an extra pick that year, in the supplemental first round, at No. 40 overall. If money hadn't been an issue, after taking Kazmir, McKeon and others would have loved to have taken Brian McCann, a left-handed hitting high school catcher from Georgia. But because they had to count their pennies and had an idea of what it would take to sign Votto, they had to come up with a money-saver in the form of University of Texas-San Antonio senior Mark Schramek, who would sign for the bargain price of just $200,000. And that set the table for the Reds to take Votto, drafted as a catcher, at No. 44 overall, the third selection in the second round.

This is the way the draft often goes, and any scouting director could play the "what if" game for eternity. This one is particularly fun, though. Had McKeon been able to take who he (and other scouts) wanted, the Reds would have walked away with Kazmir-McCann-Votto with their first three picks. Even with Kazmir's injury-interrupted career, he amassed 27.4 WAR in his career, getting traded from the Mets, who took him in the middle of the 2002 first round, to Tampa. McCann went to his hometown Braves 20 picks after the Reds took Votto, and he was a seven-time All-Star who won a World Series with Houston in 2017 and finished with 32 WAR. Add that in with Votto's 64.3 WAR through the 2022 season (second in the draft class behind only Zack Grienke) and that's a combined 124 WAR. In reality, the Reds got only Votto from that trio, with Gruler and Schramek never reaching the big leagues.

————

While all that was unfolding, Dick Groch was entrenched in the Votto household, thinking he was going to be the one to take Votto. The Yankees didn't have a first-round pick in 2002, so the first opportunity Groch would have had to take him would have been at No. 71, late in the second round. And Groch, who was still working as a special assistant for the Milwaukee Brewers into his eighties as of this writing, is 100 percent certain that had the Reds not swooped in, that's exactly who New York would have taken. The veteran scout had caught wind the Reds might be interested, so he tried to lean on the relationship he had built with Votto to make sure he ended up in pinstripes.

"I said, 'Joey, we've been with you since day one. Don't you think you owe something to the Yankees?'" Groch recalled. "And he said, 'I'll tell you what. You bring a contract and put it right in front of me now and it says New York Yankees on it, I want to sign it.' I tell him, 'Let me know when you hear back from any club.'"

A couple of days later, according to Groch, Votto tells him the Reds had indeed made contact and told him they would offer him around $550,000. McKeon remembers talking to Votto about this and that he said the Yankees would give him $600K, a number McKeon agreed verbally to match.

Groch made out a contract for that amount, ready for Votto to sign and hatched a whole plan to keep Votto away from watching the draft or paying attention to where he might go. He wanted him out of the house and off the phones, with Votto signaling that if the Reds or any other team didn't take him earlier, he was more than ready to go to the Yankees at No. 71.

"We were there, the contract was made out. He was ready to sign. Mom and Dad didn't even go to work."

Votto, for his part, was more than happy to step away from the stress of the day, thinking that he was going to be a Yankee by the end of the draft, even if he wasn't quite confident enough to believe it would come true.

"I wanted to go to school, I wanted some sense of normalcy, I didn't want to hang out there and deal with the pressure of my family and what was going on at the house," Votto said. "So I went to school. And being honest with you, before the draft, I still thought, 'Maybe 10th round pick, maybe eighth round, maybe 15th round.' And then I'll kind of decide what I want to do as far as sign professionally, but I really didn't think that I was going to go as high.

"All of a sudden, the day of, I'm over at my buddy's house after school. And we get through the first round and we're playing video games and bumming around, listening to music or whatever. And then all of a sudden, the second round kicks, I start getting some phone calls. Would you sign for this? Would you sign with us for that? Are you going to sign with us if you get picked with this slot that we're in at this spot? And I just kept saying I would really like to play pro ball, I'm interested in playing. I think [the Reds] got the sense that there was some interest in the second round from other teams and ended up taking me."

The Reds knew they had taken many by surprise, other than Groch, who had to pack up his Yankees contract and leave the Votto home, when they took Votto in the second round. So Castleberry was sent in a hurry to Toronto to sign the young hitter. The Vottos didn't have an agent and the Reds were worried with the attention that comes with a second-round selection, they would come swarming.

"One of our scouts came in the room and said, 'My buddy just said he's got Joey Votto as his client,'" McKeon said. "Well, that fired me up because Joey didn't have an agent. So somebody in that room called and put their buddy on him. And he said, 'Yeah, he's planning on flying to Toronto tomorrow. So I said,

'John, you really have to get on that plane. Get up there and get them signed.'"

"Back in those days, guys didn't know who went, but once their names were out, the agents were all over it," Castleberry said. "So that's why we wanted to get in there before. I kept calling, but the phone's busy. Finally, I got through."

Once Castleberry made contact—he had told the family he was on his way to them before he hopped on his flight—he met the family in the house and made his pitch: It's your time, your opportunity, we took you this high because we like you... a typical spiel from scout to drafted player. Castleberry initially offered a bit lower than what was talked about, again, not uncommon in terms of negotiating. At that point, the Vottos had former big leaguer Greg O'Halloran as a de facto advisor, and there was a bit of tension-inducing haggling. Finally, the two sides agreed to the below-slot $600,000 he signed for in the wee hours of the morning.

"You never want to cheat anybody out of any money," McKeon said. "That's not how I ever operated, but we only had a certain amount of budget so if you know if he was going to okay it, that was perfect, which he did, but then as soon as somebody else started getting in his ear, it might change his mind well then that would ruin the whole draft. My draft was pretty much over anyway because our money was gone. Joey was it, we were hanging our hat on Joey."

Castleberry stayed late into the night hammering out the details with Votto's late father and they had to wake Joey, who had fallen asleep on the couch, to sign on the dotted line. Castleberry was so nervous about all of it, he left his briefcase at the house and had to circle back to get it in the middle of the night. All parties can laugh about it now, but there were some tense moments.

"It was not fun, it was stressful," Votto said. "And I guess I'm sounding ungrateful, but the night was pretty stressful. I was grateful to sign professionally and it was a hefty sum of money that I was very, very lucky to receive.

"More than anything, it was like an opportunity. I felt like a door was opened and I didn't know what was on the other side. But it was a door I was willing to walk through. And one that I'd been dreaming of walking through since I was a boy and here I was living it. It's never as romantic as it sounds. Especially when you become a pro, it becomes quite a bit more serious. Which I'm fine with. I'm a more serious person anyway, so it fits my personality."

With the business side of the process taking a bit of the joy out of it, it wasn't until Votto got started on playing baseball for a living that he was able to put it behind him.

"I think that I signed for the right amount of money, but I didn't feel good until I landed in Sarasota, put the uniform on and got to work. I didn't feel good until I started swinging a bat or playing catch or seeing how great my competition is, staying at the hotel joking with teammates, eating independently. I felt free as an 18-year-old professional. It was the first time in my life that I felt free."

And it could have gone so much differently. Votto has spent his entire career in Cincinnati, quickly giving up catching and settling in as one of the best first basemen of his generation, with over 2,000 hits and 300 homers, a batting average hovering around .300 and, of course, an on-base percentage well north of .400. But what numbers could he have put up in Yankee Stadium had Dick Groch had his way? Groch, for his part, feels the left-handed hitting Votto would have taken great advantage of the short porch in right field. But Votto feels otherwise.

"I think I would have been [a] much worse hitter because of the ballpark, to be honest, with everything I've ever heard," Votto said. "There's a real emphasis on pulling the ball. And that's not a strength of mine. I think I'm glad that I didn't sign with them because I perhaps would have fallen into that sort of pull-the-ball-all-the-time approach and what changed my career was being able to hit the ball all over the field."

That hasn't stopped Votto, however, from telling Groch whenever he saw him at a ballpark to thank him for his interest and to talk about what might have been. The veteran evaluator remembers seeing Votto early on his pro career, when you might think a teenager wouldn't have the presence of mind to know what to say to the scout who *didn't* sign him.

"He comes to me across the field and he says, 'I'm sorry. I wanted to be a Yankee. I wanted it for me and for you,'" Groch said. "I laughed and said, 'Joey, guys like you, with your makeup and your simple ability to come over here and make that statement to me shows me you've got the maturity to play in the major leagues at any stadium in baseball.'"

Chapter 2

Shane Bieber

Any self-respecting sports movie fan knows the plot of *Rudy*. It's based on the real-life experience of Rudy Ruettiger, who wills his way onto the Notre Dame football team when he really has no business doing so given his size, inability to pay for school, and a lack of the grades typically needed to get in without a scholarship.

Rudy's story, and the dramatic re-telling of it starring Sean Astin, has been the quintessential underdog story for a generation. And it's provided a Hollywood-worthy definition of the term "walk-on."

Any time that term is used, it's hard not to picture some version of Rudy, a guy who works harder than everyone else, perhaps with less talent, overcoming odds to find glory on the playing field.

If the life and career of All-Star and 2020 American League Cy Young Award winner Shane Bieber is ever dramatized on screen, perhaps there will be a similar arc. He was, technically, a walk-on at the University of California Santa Barbara before being selected in the fourth round of the 2016 Major League Baseball Draft by the Cleveland Indians and making a very rapid ascent to the big leagues.

But it would have to contain one of those "based on real events" disclaimers because while Bieber certainly has become much more than anyone anticipated, his ascent isn't quite in Rudy territory.

———

If there's one Achilles heel of the scouting industry, one thing that carries too much weight, it's the radar gun. They are a constant behind home plate at any scouted game, with the velocity of each pitch from every pitching prospect recorded for future scrutiny. If a pitcher doesn't register certain numbers with his fastball, scouts will typically lose interest.

That number has changed over the years as pitchers have thrown harder and harder while younger and younger. The average velocity in MLB these days is around 92 mph and according to Statcast, of the big league pitchers who threw 50 or more pitches in 2021, 185 of them averaged 95 mph or better with their fastballs. Once upon a time, it was a rarity to hear about a pitcher reaching 100 mph at any level. It still can create oohs-and-ahhs in a crowd when the stadium radar gun hits triple digits, but it's become fairly commonplace.

That's filtered down to the amateur scene, where we've seen 100 mph on a fairly regular basis over the last several years. From high schoolers. There's a debate to be had about the long-term health of pitchers throwing that hard that young, but that's for another book. Whatever your thoughts on that topic, there's no question young hurlers are bigger and stronger than they've ever been, with velocities on mounds increasing everywhere.

In 2016, the year Bieber went in that fourth round, Riley Pint was the No. 4 pick in the draft. He was a big high schooler from Kansas who routinely hit triple digits and sat in the upper-90s. A series of injuries and continual issues with control led to him retiring from baseball at the age of 23 without having thrown a pitch above A ball in the minors, though he did return in 2022 and reached Triple-A as a relief pitcher. This is not to pick on the Rockies, who gave Pint $4.8 million to sign, but rather as a signpost for that aforementioned fascination with velocity. Truth be told, had Colorado not taken Pint, someone up very early in the first round that year would have.

The flip side of that coin is Bieber, who had a reputation as an advanced college arm who really knew how to pitch but didn't throw super hard. That's why he didn't hear his name called until pick No. 122 overall and got $420,000 to start his pro career. At the conclusion of the 2022 season, Bieber had more Wins Above Replacement (WAR), 15.3, than any other member of the 2016 Draft class.

That was after three years of growth, physically, and mentally, at the University of California Santa Barbara. He had a successful high school career, especially once he focused on baseball only. (Bieber played football for a while, but a broken wrist suffered on the gridiron helped him realize he should focus his work on the diamond.) But he typically topped out with his fastball in the 86–88 mph, albeit with a very good feel to pitch.

It's not that scouts didn't have the opportunity to see him pitch. Bieber went to Laguna Hills High School in Southern California, which can be found between Los Angeles and San Diego. While Laguna Hills isn't necessarily the professional player factory that some other SoCal schools have been, there have been a dozen pros to come from its baseball program. And the school plays against scores of other baseball powerhouses in the region.

The school sits about two-and-a-half hours south of where Bieber went to college, so the area scouts who evaluated him at Santa Barbara likely didn't see him in high school. But cross-checkers responsible for the west coast certainly could have. They largely had a similar response about that possibility, something along the lines of, *I'm sure I saw him, but I don't recall him standing out.*

Not that Bieber didn't dream of being discovered. What base-ball-playing kid didn't, and Bieber always thought that in one of those SoCal matchups, an evaluator would show up, probably to see someone else, and recognize the latent talent he had. But it never happened. A start, recounted by Bieber, against Dana Hills High School in the spring of 2013, when he could have been taken as a high school senior, really sums up how off the radar he really was:

> It was me facing off with a lefty who was a big, project-able hard-throwing lefty, Blake Taylor, ended up going in the first or second round. It was me versus him and I hyped it up. I was thinking, 'Let's go, there's going to be a lot of scouts there, this and that, it's going to be a good game.' I have a clean first inning, he comes out for the bottom of the first. And he had some control issues, throwing hard. We knocked him around a little bit, he didn't end up making it out of the first inning, and I'm on third base, because I was still hitting at the time. And I watch him get pulled out of the game, it's either the first or second inning, but early, and I see all these scouts pack their radar guns up, throw them in the bag, and just dip because, you know, they got other places to be and other guys to see that are on their list. And I was like, I just remember being on third base, thinking, 'No way. I'm out here trying to do my thing.' But at the end of the day, I wasn't popping that 90, I was maybe sitting at 86, 87, 88. And it just wasn't too sexy. So I remember standing on third base, and I was like, 'Where are you guys going? You gotta stay!' But looking back, I understand.

Laguna Hills went on to win that game and Bieber threw well, pitching into the seventh inning and allowing just one earned run (three total), walking one and striking out six. Taylor, for his part, didn't make it out of the second inning, allowing five runs on seven hits and four walks, according to MaxPreps.

Obviously, Taylor had more success than that over the course of his senior season, but the scene painted by Bieber was telling. Scouts came to see the 6′3″ lefty who was touching the mid-90s in high school and was ranked No. 61 on MLB. com's Top 100 draft prospects ranking that year, No. 55 on *Baseball America*'s Top 500. Bieber, who was listed as 6′2″, 175 pounds himself back then? He didn't appear on either list in high school. He did register on Perfect Game's (PG) rankings, coming in at No. 212… in California. Taylor was No. 10 in the state, No. 49 overall (among high schoolers), according to PG.

Taylor ended up getting drafted in the second round of that 2013 Draft, signing with the Pirates for $750,000. To his credit, he toiled away in relative anonymity in the minor leagues, had Tommy John surgery after getting traded to the Mets, gained some traction with a move to the bullpen in 2019, got traded to the Astros, and has become a valuable member of the big league relief corps, helping Houston reach the postseason in 2020 and the World Series in 2021.

Bieber went undrafted, allowing him to head to Santa Barbara undetected.

———————

The only thing Bieber was certain of as his high school career unfolded was that he really liked to pitch and wanted to find a way to keep doing it somewhere. But given the lack of eye-popping stuff, that was easier said than done. Just like pro scouts weren't bearing down on him in any way, college recruiters weren't exactly banging down his door.

There was a nibble from Santa Clara, but as a private school that wasn't offering much in the way of scholarship money, that didn't seem to make sense. Some suggested going the junior college route to continue baseball and see where that would take him, a path that has worked for many a big leaguer.

In the end, though, it was always going to be UC Santa Barbara. And the baseball was secondary. He had visited the school more than once and fell in love with the campus. He had some friends who had gone there and reported positive things about it. So, baseball or no, Santa Barbara was his school.

———

Now's the time to bust the Rudy walk-on myth.

Bieber did not show up at Coach Andrew Checketts' office, hat in hand, offering to wash uniforms and serve as a groundskeeper just to get his foot in the baseball program's door. He had been seen as a high schooler, first as a junior who was throwing only about 80–82 mph with that excellent feel for pitching. He went to a team camp on campus the summer before his senior year and it was more of the same: topping out at 83 mph, but making hitters look bad and filling up the strike zone, albeit with slightly below-average stuff overall.

"There still wasn't enough velocity where we said, 'Yeah, we really want to do it,'" Checketts said as he looked through his old recruiting notes.

One of Checketts' assistants at the time, Jason Hawkins, saw Bieber one other time and even though he still wasn't throwing much harder, Hawkins felt Bieber's projectable body and feel for pitching were worth bringing him to campus.

"We bought him on layaway," Checketts said. "We were low on money. At that point, we were late in the recruiting cycle. It was hard to [squeeze anymore money out]. If we knew he was going to be a Cy Young Award winner, we would've squeezed some money in there right then. But we didn't know. So he wanted to go to school, Santa Barbara was somewhere he wanted to go. So, we said we'll give you an opportunity and if you perform and do well and work hard, your second year we'll have a scholarship for you. The first year, we're pretty much tapped out at this point. And he committed to that."

So maybe that doesn't lead fans to chant Bie-ber, Bie-ber, or get the custodian played by Charles S. Dutton to raise a fist in his air in triumph, but that's kind of how it all started.

Bieber figured he'd get a good education and the school is on the beach, so if baseball didn't work out, he'd get a good degree from the school, which was part of the UC public school system (read: not nearly as costly as Santa Clara) he wanted to attend. It was kind of no-lose for him at the time. The unofficial term was "preferred walk-on," where the baseball program would help him get into the school but without a scholarship from the get-go.

"I had like borderline grades, and I had been working towards it," Bieber said. "They said that's one of the perks, they get me into school. And I was like, 'Well, if I'm going to Santa Barbara, I guess I'm kind of playing with house money. I'm going to keep playing baseball as long as I can. If I don't make the team, then then so be it.' But obviously, things ended up working out a little bit differently."

It didn't happen overnight, though Bieber had added enough strength before his freshman year that he was up to around 86–88 mph with his fastball by the time he was ready to set foot on campus. That's far from eye-opening and while his appearance on campus was not movie script fodder, it was true that he did not have a guaranteed spot on the Gauchos' pitching staff.

Kids with scholarships would get first preference and likely more chances to show they belonged on the roster. Bieber had a couple of things working in his favor before he even had one fall practice.

The first was who *wasn't* heading to campus. Tyler Mahle was another high school pitcher from Southern California, one who had some similarities to Bieber at the time: a lack of premium stuff velocity, but an athletic and projectable body. He also had better present secondary stuff with his curve and changeup than Bieber had in 2013. Most felt Mahle would head to Santa Barbara especially because his older brother Greg would be a junior left-handed reliever there that year. But the Cincinnati Reds took the young right-hander in the seventh round of the 2013 Draft and gave him $250,000—nearly $90,000 more than the bonus amount suggested by MLB—to sign him away from his college commitment. In Bieber's eyes, that opened a slot for him to make the team, or at the very least took away one less player to compete against.

The second was that Bieber sort of fit a mold that Checketts clearly liked to have on his staff. He and the other coaches weren't afraid of bringing in a strike-thrower who didn't throw hard or have that good of a breaking ball. They'd done it before, with some of those pitchers on the staff Bieber would join, so they were willing to give Bieber the chance to do so.

"There's not that security, but one good thing about the position that I was in was that I was a pitcher, and we always need innings in the fall, like you're trying to scrimmage, scrimmage, scrimmage," Bieber said. "So, I got my opportunities versus an outfielder or hitter. They're in the third lineup or whatever, they may not get as many [at bats]. I'm going out there and I'm throwing I'm trying to throw well, and as long as you continue to throw well, you're going to get more opportunities and more innings and fortunately, that's the way things kind of worked out."

When Bieber arrived, Matt Harvey was in his third year with Santa Barbara. No, not the Matt Harvey who was a Mets first-round pick. THAT Matt Harvey was a National League All-Star in 2013, the year Bieber graduated from high school. THIS Matt Harvey had been a student and bullpen catcher at the University of Nebraska and was heading west to be a volunteer coach at Westmont, a small NAIA college in California, when a connection landed him at Santa Barbara as an administrative assistant. After a year of what Harvey calls "following Coach Checketts around," he was able to start helping on the field as an assistant strength and conditioning coach. His third year was Bieber's first, and he moved into a pitching coach kind of role after that, so he got to grow with Bieber.

"It was in the program's blood a little bit at that time that you could have a guy not throw a 92-mph fastball with a hammer breaking ball and have success," said Harvey, who is now the pitching coach at UC San Diego. "So I think that helped shape the view of Bieber when he showed up is that we'd seen this work.

"When he showed up, it was under-average velo, but the command tool was really good. The fastball had a little bit of a wrinkle to it. It was less of the jump that it has now and more sink and run, which really plays in college baseball, if you can throw that at the bottom of the zone and throw a fastball away. I mean, 80 percent of the fastballs or more in college baseball are away and down. He showed the ability to do that really well early on."

Because he was throwing only around 86 mph at that point and was around 6′2″ and maybe 170 pounds, one of the key things was for him to add strength to that frame while getting all those fall innings in.

"From day one, he knew how to work," Harvey said. "And when he had a baseball in his hand, that was when he was clearly the most comfortable. So his throwing, his bullpens, it all looked the part. It didn't have the requisite velocity and stuff to go with it. The major development stuff for him was getting bigger and stronger."

Bieber had some good models to follow in the strike-throwing mold right from the get-go. Austin Pettibone had a similar frame and similar stuff (below-average fastball velocity, not much of a breaking ball). He also had some big league bloodlines, with his older brother Jonathan making it up with the Phillies in 2013–14 and their dad Jay spending six years in pro ball, including a cup of coffee with the Minnesota Twins in 1983. Bieber basically shadowed Pettibone, likely to be the school's ace in the spring, all fall, and into the spring. Even watching him go out and pitch was a how-to in getting hitters at that level out with the stuff they had.

And Pettibone was far from the only pro prospect on the team. He would get drafted in the 24th round of the draft that spring (2014) and go on to play for five summers in the Texas Rangers organization. Greg Mahle, Tyler's older brother, was a bullpen workhorse that spring who was taken by the Los Angeles Angels in the 15th round of the '14 Draft. Justin Jacome was a sophomore starter taken by the Marlins in the fifth round of the 2015 Draft. And the most famous name on that staff, at least in terms of draft prospect circles, was Dillon Tate. He was the Gauchos' closer in 2014, with power stuff, and it was a move into the rotation in 2015 that landed him as the No. 4 overall pick of that June's draft. Lefty Andrew Vasquez ended up transferring from UCSB to Westmont for his senior season in 2015, went in the 32nd round in that draft. He, Tate, and Mahle from this deep crop have all seen at least some time in the major leagues. The 2016 staff Bieber led had several other pros, with Kyle Nelson, then a sophomore, joining Bieber in the big leagues.

All of this to say there were scores of talented pitchers for Bieber to watch, learn from, pick the brains of. And he had a coaching staff, led by Andrew Checketts, to help shepherd him along the way. In a short amount of time, Checketts, who pitched a year at the University of Florida and then three at Oregon State, had built up a strong reputation as a pitching coach and recruiter at UC Riverside and Oregon before landing the head coaching gig after the 2011 season. By 2013, the Gauchos had reached postseason play, competing in an NCAA Regional for the first time in a dozen years. Santa Barbara hosted a regional in 2015 and went to the College World Series in 2016, with Bieber as its ace. That 2015 team set a school record for team ERA and strikeouts.

Bieber threw well enough in the fall and the lead up to the spring 2014 season to land a spot somewhere in the rotation. Two things helped pave the way. Vasquez didn't throw as well as expected or hoped. The big lefty had a very promising freshman year in 2012, less so in 2013 and only tossed 20 innings in 2014, one of the reasons he left for Westmont for his senior season.

While Bieber was outpitching Vasquez, his mentor Pettibone was on the shelf to start the spring season. A shoulder issue kept him off the mound for the first month-plus of the season. At the very least, that opened a window for Bieber to audition in the weekend rotation, a plum assignment for a freshman, especially one with no scholarship. He pitched well enough to be the Gauchos' Sunday starter, showing off how often he found the strike zone—he walked just 1.5 per nine in 11 starts—and how often he found too much of the strike zone—he gave up 10.9 hits per nine. He also only struck out 5.6 per nine that year, an indication that his stuff, while better than during his high school days, was far from over-powering, with Harvey estimating he was throwing his fastball in the 85–88 mph range on average.

Overall, it was a solid first season for Bieber, finishing with a 3.76 ERA over those 11 starts and that low K rate was kind of in line with the entire staff, which struck out just 6.79 per nine for the season, yet managed to go 34–17–1. And he did it more or less by commanding his fastball and not much else.

"I remember a moment where he was getting ready to play against Cal Poly," said Checketts, referencing an April 6 start Bieber would lose, 1–0. "He was warming up in the pen. And we were still working on the breaking ball. And we're mid-season now, we're still every week trying to hammer out how to get this breaking ball better because he was pretty much a one-pitch pitcher. He had kind of a show me slurve at that point. And I remember specifically him warming up in the pen and me telling him, 'Hey, you can beat everybody with just fastballs,' because he was bouncing a bunch of breaking balls and struggling with it. He threw a really good game and threw a lot of fastballs there.

"So that was his first year, it was pretty much all fastballs and then the secondary stuff got a little bit better second year, and then the velocity started to come. And then by his third year, he was really commanding it well. Still a lot of fastballs, but the secondary stuff was better."

Physical, not to mention pitching, maturation can happen at different times for different people. It's not uncommon for a young pitcher to make a large step forward in those 18–20 years. Bieber's was definitely more of a gradual progression.

"He learned a lot about having a routine and the mentality in the game that is required if you're going to succeed with less stuff than maybe some of the other guys have," Harvey said about his freshman year. "And then every year just got a little bit bigger and a little bit stronger. And through his junior year, he was up like 30 pounds from when he showed up on campus. And that's no surprise with the velo increase and all that."

As a sophomore, Bieber was probably closer to the 87–90 mph range consistently and by his junior year he really was around 90–93 mph more often than not. It was during that second year of serving again as Santa Barbara's Sunday starter that Bieber thinks was a turning point, not only in terms of how he performed, but in terms of thinking about a future beyond college.

"I consider probably my best year in terms of growth was my sophomore season," Bieber said. "Not only did I start throwing a little bit harder, because I was finally on a college weight program, meal program, and all that stuff. But I was learning quite a bit from Dillon Tate, Justin Jacome. James Carter that year was in our bullpen before he got Tommy John surgery and he was lights out. And a bunch of other pitchers I'm sure I'm leaving out."

All three pitchers in that weekend rotation, Tate, Jacome, and Bieber, topped 100 innings for the year as the Gauchos posted a team ERA of 2.45, a very large reason why the team went 40–17 and hosted an NCAA Regional (though they were unable to advance). Tate pitched his way to the top of the first round, Jacome went in the fifth.

"That starting staff… That was fun. That was a really fun year. I had grown a lot, physically and mentally. But also it was my first season where I ever actually put up pretty damn good numbers."

Pretty damn good numbers, indeed. Bieber finished with a 2.24 ERA over his 112⅔ innings of work, leading that impressive staff. His hit rate went down to 9.1 per nine, he was stingy as ever in giving up free passes (1.0/9) and he even missed more bats, striking out 7.6 per nine. In 2015, the steps forward weren't as much from seeing how a similar pitcher like Pettibone did things, but rather finding other lessons from Tate, who MLB.com ranked as the No. 5 prospect in that entire draft class and who cranked his fastball up to 98 mph, and Jacome, a 6′6″ lefty.

"I learned a lot about myself," Bieber said. "I still wasn't striking a lot of guys out, but I was going deep into ball games on Sundays. And those are usually the rubber match games and big games and I appreciated that. What was fun about that starting staff and us three, we always pushed each other, we were always talking smack, we were always learning from each other, three very different pitchers. But we were able to pick and choose and kind of pick each other's brains and learn what makes each other tick. And try to take the goods from each other."

––––––––

As far as Bieber had come over two years at Santa Barbara and the 27 appearances he made, it was three starts across the country that may have really changed the trajectory of his career. There are college summer leagues all over the United States, but the cream of the crop, the gold standard, is the Cape Cod League.

For years, the Cape Cod League has attracted the best college talent to New England each summer, the majority of whom will be college juniors the following spring. It's a wood-bat league, meaning scouts who come get to see top draft-eligible talent in competition that is a closer facsimile of the pro game. One of the biggest challenges in scouting amateurs has been projecting how skills will translate from the metal bats of years ago or the composite bats used today collegiately to the wood-bat action of the next level.

Evaluators come in droves to help get a sense of who the key players in the college class are for the following draft. And who doesn't want to spend a week or two on the Cape while doing so?

Shane Bieber really wanted to spend some time there because he knew that's where someone who wanted to get drafted needed to go to be seen. Something in the right-hander had changed during that outstanding sophomore year, both on the field and off. And while he was maturing, he also saw a lot of good pitching talent in the Big West Conference.

Chief among those was Thomas Eshelman, a right-handed starter from Cal State Fullerton. Bieber saw a lot of himself in

Eshelman, who was about as extreme a strike-thrower Division I baseball has seen in recent years. A three-year starter, Eshelman finished his college career with a 1.65 ERA and an absolutely ridiculous 0.4 walks per nine rate. In 2015, Eshelman shut out Santa Barbara for eight innings when the two schools met each other, and he walked just seven in 137 innings that year en route to being a second-round pick of the Astros in that June's draft.

Bieber saw some similar qualities, while recognizing Eshelman at the time was a step ahead of him: despite not having premium stuff, filling up the strike zone. Seeing someone like him get drafted definitely planted a seed and made his desire to compete in the Cape even stronger.

There was just one thing keeping that from happening: his workload. Bieber had thrown 112⅔ innings during his sophomore year, more than double his total in 2014 and there was genuine concern about throwing too much. Everyone involved saw the value in him going, but some bargaining had to take place.

"I had thrown quite a bit my sophomore season," Bieber recalled. "I had committed to go to the Cape, I knew it was probably going to be instrumental in my development, my exposure more than anything. And Coach Checketts, he was worried about my arm and how much I'd been working and throwing.

"And so we ended up cutting a deal, basically. I was supposed to go for the whole year, but they ended up making me a temp. And I was there for a couple weeks."

Checketts had developed a strong relationship with Scott Pickler, the manager for Yarmouth-Dennis in the Cape Cod League. Justin Jacome had gone from UCSB to Y-D the previous summer and the two coaches had mutual trust and respect for one another. So they made sure they were on the same page in terms of how Bieber could be used.

"Andrew said, 'Hey, the kid really wants to go out there. He's a competitor,'" said Pickler, who has been at the helm of Yarmouth-Dennis for a quarter-century. "And being in Southern California, I knew who he was. And so he said, 'We're going to let him go out there and make three or four starts for him and see what happens.' And I knew I was getting a competitor. I knew he was a good kid, because I checked with Andrew and he said, 'You're going to love this kid.' And I loved him when he got there and loved the way he competed."

It turned out to be three starts, a grand total of 18⅔ innings. After a brief amount of time getting ramped back up—his last college outing had been a rough relief outing on May 30—Bieber made his first Cape start on June 19, a solid five-inning effort during which he gave up two runs (one earned) on three hits and struck out five, while of course walking only one.

Start number two, on June 26, is the one that stands out for a number of reasons. The line was impressive enough: 7⅔ innings, no runs, four hits, one walk, and eight strikeouts. Beyond the box score was Bieber showing just how competitive he is on the mound.

Yarmouth-Dennis took an early 1–0 lead and Bieber made it stand up. Keep in mind, he was on a strict innings and pitch count, so the time came for Pickler to remove him from the game. Now Pickler's no novice, he's had countless big leaguers come his way, and says Bieber reminded him of Walker Buehler and his competitiveness, which he had seen firsthand the year prior, in 2014. He was accustomed to pitchers not wanting to come out of a game, especially when it's a tight contest, even in the laid-back Cape.

"I don't let those guys usually go over 75 pitches," Pickler said. "And you know, there's times that I go out to the mound. And I say, 'Hey, that's it.' And these kids fight with me and tell me no and things like that. I'm sure I went out there near the

75 mark and I said, 'Hey, that's it.' And he talked me out of it. That doesn't happen very often. But I said, 'You're going to call Checketts if we go too many more pitches.'"

"Yeah, he's competitive," Checketts said with a chuckle. "So we were tracking it closely and I had a lot of faith and trust in Scott Pickler. We had had a lot of conversations about how this is good for him, it's good for his profile, it's good to be scouted, it's good for him to have that experience and see himself as one of those guys. So we want him to go, but he's got a lot of innings on his arm from the year before with us. And so the plan all along was to get to a certain number of innings, and then send him home after that.

"I can see a little bit of a stretch there at the end, where the innings went up a little bit. He's competitive and he's always had a history of being healthy. So we weren't sweating it a whole lot. I can't remember if he was begging to stay longer, he probably was."

He made just one more start, but honestly, he didn't need to after this gem. That's largely because Jason Smith was at this masterpiece. And Smith at the time was the West Coast cross-checker for the Cleveland Indians who had headed to the Cape to check in on some players of interest from out West against the competition only the Cape Cod League could offer.

The scouting pyramid becomes a bit inverted during the summer. During the school year, it's typically the area scout who creates a "follow list" of players in the fall, the group of prospects worth tracking come the regular season. It's the area scout who gives a list to his or her cross-checker of higher priority guys to check out.

But in the summer, it can be reversed. An area scout in California isn't as likely to head across the country, but all 30 teams scout the Cape Cod League heavily, and in addition to New England area scouts, cross-checkers, and scouting directors will go to take in some action.

Smith started scouting for Cleveland in 2001 as an area scout, first in Southern California, then the central part of the state. He got promoted up to West Coast cross-checker in advance of the 2013 Draft. So when Smith, who moved on to become a national cross-checker for the Los Angeles Angels for the 2017 draft season, landed in the Cape, it was after his third Draft in the supervisory role. He knew of Bieber as a guy who could throw strikes and not throw very hard, but had never evaluated him on the mound and he was on a list of West Coast guys he wanted to see during his stay.

Smith's first order of business was to check in with his contacts to find out who was playing where and who was pitching when. High up on the list, of course, was the veteran Cape manager, Pickler, who told him he had to come check out Bieber. And when Scott Pickler tells you to come see a player, a good scout listens.

Pickler had told Smith that Bieber was on a bit of a tight leash, that he was going to go five innings at the most, as per his agreement with Checketts.

"The Cape is really the first under-the-microscope look at Shane for me," Smith said. "I'm watching him pitch and he was good. He's what everyone probably said he was, kind of 88–91. He was kind of moving it moving the fastball in and out, he was missing bats. He didn't always get to the slider, but he had one in there. And he had a good changeup that got him through five innings."

At this point, Smith remembers Bieber running into a little trouble in the fifth and figures he's seen all of Bieber he's going to see when Pickler headed to the mound, so he starts figuring out if he can make it to another game to catch some other players on his list. He grabs his bag to leave, then sees Pickler return to the dugout.

"I'm thinking, 'Oh, okay, he's going to let him work through this a little bit,'" Smith recalled. "He got out of a jam and thought for sure that would be it. As I'm walking out towards the line, Bieber comes back out for the sixth."

After taking in a scoreless sixth, Smith heads for his car, until…

"He came back out in the seventh! And I thought, 'Oh my gosh, Pick, you're going to get in trouble. You'll never get a Santa Barbara guy again. You're over-throwing these kids, and they're going to find out about it.'"

Smith remembers vividly that Bieber reached back for 93 mph on his fastball in that seventh frame and that he pitched with more intent. It was valuable information he stored, though he didn't hold back when he saw Pickler the next day.

"'Pick what are you doing? You can't throw these guys like that!' And he said he wouldn't let me take him out. There was no way he was coming out. So that showed some toughness, some grit to him. And some willingness, you know, to have a mature conversation with an adult, the manager of a Cape team and say, 'No, I got this.'"

"I've always had a little bit of a chip on my shoulder," Bieber said. "But I'm realistic about things and I know the exposure at Santa Barbara isn't great. West Coast ball is a lot different than East Coast ball and getting out to the Cape was something that was really important to me. So I end up bargaining for three starts and I'm going to go make the most of them. So I think that's where my head was at when at some point Pick comes out and says, 'You're done,' and I was asking for more."

———

That information found its way into the notes Smith passed along on his follow report. It's standard for scouts to put follows into one of two buckets, simply "low follow" or "high follow." A low follow means it's someone to see if he gets better during the year and thus makes him more of a draft target. A high follow is for a player a scout wants to say, "Hey, we should really focus on this guy." After that one start on the Cape, Bieber fit into the latter category according to Smith. And that's a big reason why he and area scout Carlos Muniz drove up to Santa Barbara's campus to interview Bieber that fall.

This is a part of the scouting gig many people don't know about, and it's become more and more important. Given the financial and resources expenditure on top draftees, teams want to get a strong sense of a player's makeup and character. Muniz had seen Bieber during fall ball—most colleges, at the very least, have a Scout's Day—and was immediately impressed with Bieber's command and how he carried himself, even if he admitted he didn't have a true out pitch at the time.

Muniz, who began scouting for Cleveland in 2013, had an area that stretches from Long Beach, just south of Los Angeles, up to Cal Poly San Luis Obispo, over to Bakersfield, and back down. That's just under 500 miles if you drive it in a perimeter. Even by the fourth draft in 2016, he'd had some success. The first player he ever signed was Adam Plutko, a right-hander with a very good feel to pitch (sound familiar?) out of UCLA, taken in the 11th round of the 2013 Draft. Plutko would make his big league debut in September of 2016, just a couple of months after Cleveland selected Bieber. And he's had a handful of other players he's drafted at least touched the bigs.

But what might have made Muniz the perfect scout to evaluate Bieber was his own playing background. He was a slightly under-sized right-hander taken in Round 13 of the 2003 Draft by the Mets out of Long Beach State. A reliever who closed at Long Beach in 2003, he had to prove himself at every level and eventually made it up to help the bullpen in New York in 2007 and 2008. That might not sound like much, but given the astronomical odds for someone taken that late in the draft to make it to the highest level even for a day, it's quite an achievement. And it certainly helped form his baseball worldview in terms of scouting.

"The road wasn't paved for me," Muniz said. "I was pretty much in the trenches throughout my career, battling, and I saw the game differently compared to guys who pretty much had it handed to them. I had to work extra. That side of the game, I see it differently."

Muniz, armed with that perspective and what he saw in the fall, and Smith, with his glowing report from the Cape, arrived in Santa Barbara clearly wanting to like Bieber. And he wasn't disappointed.

The meeting took place outside of a Starbucks right off-campus during a time Bieber described as "rush hour" with tons of students walking, or on bikes and skateboards. Muniz and Smith settle into a table and watch the hustle and bustle of the Santa Barbara student body waiting for Bieber to arrive.

According to Muniz, Bieber comes in on his bike, wearing flip-flops, quite the norm at UCSB. And then proceeds to lead a master class about pitching that still blows Muniz away while the two Cleveland scouts tried to challenge him to answer tough questions.

"To this day, it's one of the best player meetings I've ever had," Muniz said. "It was as if you were talking to a seasoned major league pitcher with 10 years under his belt. From the way he prepared before a game, the way he analyzed the scouting report, complete feel for his pitches and an advanced feel of understanding his strengths and weaknesses. Shane was pretty much driven and, at that time, he had a positive mindset. It was a special moment."

"In interviewing a player, we try not to take things at face value," Smith said. "I know it's hard for a scout because we're meeting with him, we drove three-and-a-half hours to get there,

there's a lot involved, we like the player. So, when we ask questions, the tendency is to lean towards just being nice and letting him answer the questions as scripted as he wants, but we really didn't let him do that. And you can't fake that. So we knew he was genuine based off of those things. He was giving us very detailed answers of his development, his relationship with players, coaching staff, things he's learned, his aptitude, athleticism. Stuff you just can't make up."

The impression Bieber made went beyond just his answers. It was his ability to not get sidetracked by his surroundings. Bieber claimed that as a student there, you didn't notice things like this, but Smith and Muniz had to work hard to not be distracted by all of the beautiful people among the student body going by them.

"I remember it being very distracting for me and for Carlos because we had to ask tough questions and we needed answers," Smith said. "And he was very focused, he was very on point with his questions. So we knew that if you can deal with this—hundreds of kids, riding bikes, yelling at him, girls walking by in bikinis and all that, if you can answer these tough questions for a major league team, he was probably going to have some focus."

"We're outside this whole time, lunchtime rolls around, and the sorority girls are walking around with bikini tops, and they just keep walking by us," Muniz recalled. "And they're smiling. And this whole time, Shane wasn't even fazed. He was locked in the conversation. And I was like, 'Wow.' After the meeting, I told Jason 'Hey, man, this is our guy right here.'"

There was some mutual admiration going on. While Bieber would go on to meet with other teams, especially once his junior season got underway, this was really the first sit down he had with a team. And he could tell this wasn't just a couple of scouts checking names off of to-do list. They were interested and so was he.

"I just remember those guys being really cool guys, the first guys that enjoyed how I pitch," Bieber said. "They saw a little bit of the intangibles, and they appreciated me for knowledge of the game and the way I competed and some other things like that, and they never knocked it for me being 91–92 or not popping 95s or 96s like everybody else.

"So I appreciate Los and Jason for believing in me and being those guys that came to me and gave me encouragement. Those two specifically were two of the first guys that I sat down with. That was kind of my first experience in that setting. And I could tell that if the path led down that road, and I ended up going to the Indians, that I was going to be in a good spot."

———

Now it's not like the Indians scouting staff reserved a spot in the top five rounds right after that meeting. Muniz and Smith were in agreement that Bieber had some serious makeup, smarts, and the drive to maximize the tools he had. But that meeting was in November. Bieber still had to go out, stay healthy, and perform.

He had moved up and was the Gauchos' Friday night starter that spring, their ace. If there were any questions how he'd perform, he went out and tossed seven innings in the season opener, allowing two runs on seven hits and one walk, while striking out four. He would go on to pitch at least into the seventh inning in all but one of his starts (the exception was a six-inning win). He gave up more than three earned runs in just three of them and recorded five complete games, finishing with a 2.74 ERA, and while he still wasn't missing a ton of bats (7.3 K/9), he was as stingy as ever with the walks (1.1 per nine). He headed up a staff that helped Santa Barbara win 43 games and make its first-ever trip to the College World Series in Omaha.

During that postseason run, Bieber showed that competitiveness that stood out to Smith when he pitched for Yarmouth-
Dennis. Over three starts, he gave up four earned runs in 22⅓
innings. That's a 1.61 ERA and it included beating Louisville's
Brendan McKay, who was the No. 4 overall pick in the draft
that June, in the Super Regional to help stamp the Gauchos
ticket to Omaha. Those heroics came after Cleveland had already
used their fourth-round pick on him, further cementing that the
organization had made the right call.

Not that they didn't do their due diligence. Muniz thinks he
saw Bieber make five starts. Smith, as a cross-checker, couldn't
check in as much, but recalls seeing him twice, and both times he
was good. He was checking off all the boxes and Muniz was all
in, especially since it was not a strong spring for college pitching
in the area. There were some highly regarded high school hitters,
with Mickey Moniak going No. 1 overall to the Phillies and Blake
Rutherford going late in the first to the Yankees. Both were high
school outfielders. Muniz's college list? Bieber topped it.

"Shane was my guy," Muniz said. "On the collegiate side, he
was my number one guy in that area. There wasn't really a heavy
crop of college pitching and if there was, for us it was Shane
Bieber. Shane Bieber was that gut-feel guy for me."

Gut feel with a ton of looks, each time checking to see how
Bieber's stuff held up. He long had shown an ability to command the baseball, but there would be velocity dips here and
there over the course of his previous seasons. In his junior year,
his stuff held up more often than not, touching 92–93 mph
early and still sitting 89 mph late in games. Nothing Muniz
saw detracted him.

"That's plenty good, man," Muniz said. "If you can command the zone at 88–89 and get outs, with the delivery that
that kid had? It's good enough. But other guys, they would be
like, 'Ehhh, it's kind of vanilla.' I like vanilla, man. You just

put some whipped cream, nuts, and chocolate and you've got yourself a banana split."

Muniz was decidedly ahead of the industry on this one. As the draft approached, MLB.com had Bieber ranked No. 150 on its Top 200 draft prospects list. That's about the fifth round, talent-wise. *Baseball America* put him at No. 184, more in Round 6 territory. Not that those rankings are the be-all, end-all, but the general consensus was that Bieber was a Round 5–6 type talent. Bieber, for his part, had met with most teams as the year went on and he knew he needed to perform to get there or go even earlier, as he still had that Eshelman comp in his head.

"I don't need to know what these teams are saying, because I have to go out there and I have to pitch, I have to put up good numbers, first and foremost," Bieber said. "And then once we get to the draft, it can be fickle. And my strategy at the end of the day, after talking about it and learning about how the draft works… teams asked for your number and where you want to go and this and that. And I gave them the comp Eshelman. Most people kind of smirked at it. But at the end of the day, I was like, 'If I'm there, take me, because I don't want to fall down. If you think I'm worth it, and you like me, take me because at the end of the day, that's going to put me in the best position and the team is going to be more invested in me. And so, there was a lot going on, but I kind of wanted to stay blind to it in a sense, because at the end of the day, the biggest thing in front of me was to go out there and pitch well. And then if I do that, the rest will unfold and take care of itself."

If it had been up to Muniz, his club probably would have taken Bieber in Eshelman territory, in the second. But area scouts don't call the shots. Cleveland took two high school hitters, Georgia area outfielder Will Benson and Pennsylvania prep infielder Nolan Jones, in the top two rounds. The Indians used their comp round pick after the second on Oregon State catcher

Logan Ice. In the third, they took a similar college arm from the East Coast in Aaron Civale, out of Northeastern, who joined Bieber in the big league rotation in 2019. This made Muniz sweat more than a little.

"I was nervous, man" Muniz said. "I was like, 'Oh god, he's not going to be there. What's going on here?' But then he fell on our lap and we were we were so lucky we got him in the fourth round. I was excited once we took Shane Bieber. I was thrilled, regardless of if it was 88–91. I was so happy because I trusted that guy and I trusted his makeup."

"It felt about right to me," Checketts said. "I wasn't in all of the internal conversations, and the scouts don't really tip their hands a lot. It didn't surprise me, and he was one of the better pitchers in a really good conference. And the better pitchers in our conference go in the top five rounds traditionally, so that that part of it didn't surprise me."

All of this was happening while Santa Barbara was playing in the postseason. The Gauchos had won the Regional in Nashville, hosted by Vanderbilt, and were preparing for the Super Regionals hosted by Louisville.

"The draft was actually a crazy time," Bieber said. "It was like a day or two before I had to pitch in that Friday Super Regional, as well as, Santa Barbara is on a quarter system, so we had finals going on. Yeah, it was brutal. It was miserable.

"So it was just a total kind of shitstorm. To be honest, there was a bunch going on, I was stressed. And it kind of flew by because we had so much going on. But on top of finals, getting that call, getting drafted… I got the call while I was on Louisville's field for a practice, I think a day or two days before the Friday game, with finals going down that night. At the end of the day, I'm thankful for [agent Dennis Wyrick], who mediated everything. I just told him if a team wants me, tell them to take me, let's just keep it simple."

The call came while he was stretching on the field. Bieber's phone blew up and his teammates swarmed him to celebrate. But there wasn't a lot of time to revel in the moment.

"I was like, 'Shit, we have a game in like 24 hours and we have a chance of winning.' And so we ended up winning that Friday and then walking off on that Saturday as well end up going to Omaha. So it was a special, special week for sure."

––––––––

Santa Barbara's run ended on June 22. Bieber signed with the Indians six days later and signed for $420,000, just over $80K below slot value. After throwing 134⅔ innings in college that year, he pitched briefly, but well, in his summer pro debut. Things took off from there. Bieber continued to throw harder, he pitched across three levels in 2017, his first full season of pro ball. His slider got tighter, though that wasn't going to be enough. He wanted to wrinkle in a curve, what he thought would be kind of a slow breaking ball he could get over for strike one to give hitters a different look.

During his first offseason in pro ball, he was living with Trevor Bettencourt, a reliever who had transferred from Tennessee to Santa Barbara for that 2016 season and threw well enough to get drafted in Round 25 by the Phillies that June. He was very good in the postseason and Bieber remembered his absolutely nasty breaking ball. It was a spike curve and as the two former college teammates played catch, Bieber asked Betancourt to show him how he threw it.

"We played catch for the better part of an offseason," Bieber said. "And so I was able to develop that thing just a little bit, gain a little bit more feel for it each and every day, [but I still] struggled with it. And then eventually brought it to the Indians, told them about it, started throwing with... Brady Aiken and

Aaron Civale, and they started helping me out with their curve-balls, and Civ has always been able to spin it. So we just had a good time, but started developing this curveball. My thoughts for it were a lot different than [they are] now. But I'm very happy with where it's at now, and it's kind of become my baby. And I rely on it pretty heavily. But that was something that started with Trevor Betancourt. And you know, with the help of a bunch more teammates along the way, it's become what it's become."

That curve ball has become the out pitch many thought he was lacking in college. And his velocity has climbed, with a fastball that can sit in the mid-90s, to go along with a cutter, a slider, and a changeup. He is a much different pitcher than when he first walked onto campus in Santa Barbara. It can take a village to create a big league pitcher, something Bieber eagerly recognizes. But he gets the lion share of the credit, for taking in all those lessons and becoming a much better pitcher than anyone anticipated, an All Star in 2019 and 2021, and a Cy Young Award winner in the shortened 2020 season. Which begs the question: Are major league teams missing out when tossing a pitcher aside because he doesn't hit a certain benchmark veloc-ity-wise as an amateur?

"I don't want to tell Major League Baseball how to do their jobs," Checketts said. "I think command and feel is a skill and it takes time to develop it. And it's a difficult skill to develop. I think it's a combination, and everybody's greedy, they want the guy that has some feel and can develop a secondary and throws 100. And I don't think they have to give up on the radar gun. I think if you only look at the radar gun [you're in trouble, because] there are a lot of guys that throw 95-plus that aren't having successful major league careers because they don't throw enough strikes, or they don't have a feel for secondary. And so I think there just has to be a balance and a trade-off."

Even those who believed in Bieber, from Harvey to Checketts in college, to Muniz and Smith on the scouting side, couldn't have predicted what Bieber would become. And the All-Star big leaguer has never forgotten where he came from and who believed in him. When he won Cy Young honors in 2020, he was having a celebration with his family at home and Muniz called him. Not only did Bieber take the call, he also put the area scout on speaker so he could more publicly thank him for being the guy who helped him get this all started.

"Definitely humble beginnings," Smith said. "Of course, we knew what he came from as an overachiever and a walk on, and someone that was going to persevere and be a winner. And to still keep in touch with Carlos, it's a testament to who he is as a person."

Perhaps Bieber would love to be an example of why teams should look beyond the radar guns more consistently. But even he couldn't have predicted what he's been able to achieve in a relatively short amount of time.

"If you would have told me my sophomore year where I'd be at right now just a few years later, I probably would have laughed," Bieber said.

"And I guess in a way, looking back, I'm very grateful for the way that my development happened. I learned how to pitch early and then continued to work towards velo, getting bigger and stronger. And eventually that comes on the latter half. I feel like I wouldn't trade that path for anything, but it definitely was frustrating."

Chapter 3

Jacob deGrom

Jacob deGrom thinks he's a shortstop, and he always has. Pitchers hitting in the National League may now be mostly extinct, but the Mets, or whomever deGrom suits up for, may want to keep him in the lineup. He might be one of the most dominant right-handed pitchers in a generation, but when he's in the batter's box, he still fancies himself a position player. The fact he has three career big league home runs and a career .204 batting average through 2021 does give him some hitting bona fides.

The two Cy Young Awards, Rookie of the Year and four All-Star nods, however, obviously came from his exploits on the mound. But if it hadn't been for a desperate need for arms at Stetson University, he may have never collected all of that hardware.

"It's crazy when you think about it, because you don't know what would have happened [if I had stayed at shortstop]," deGrom said in a 2015 interview with the *Orlando Sentinel*. "I might not be here today."

To be fair, deGrom actually *was* a shortstop, and nothing else, when he began his college career. And he was the poster child for local kid staying home to make good. Born in DeLand, Florida, about 40 minutes north of Orlando, deGrom was an excellent athlete who starred in both basketball and baseball at Calvary Christian Academy, about a half-hour northeast of his hometown in Ormond Beach, not far from Daytona.

"He was so naturally gifted that it almost seemed effortless to him," said Ryan Knernschield, who coached deGrom in basketball at Ormond Beach Calvary Christian, in that same 2015 piece on deGrom in the *Orlando Sentinel.* "A lot of athletes had to really work hard—I am not saying he didn't work hard—but honestly he didn't have to work as hard because he could do anything.

"Golf, basketball, baseball, just everything. Great hand-eye coordination. Patient. He had just a beautiful jumper."

While he received accolades like being first-conference and helping his American Legion team win a state title one summer, he wasn't the type of elite-level player who went to the big showcase events attended by scouts. And he wasn't heavily recruited as a tall, gangly middle infielder. The one place he found a spot, and a scholarship, was in his backyard: Stetson University in DeLand.

For nearly four decades, Pete Dunn was synonymous with Stetson baseball. Dunn had caught for two years at Stetson as a player and tried his hand at professional baseball when the Kansas City Royals selected him late in the 1970 Draft. He spent two summers in the low levels of the minors before realizing that wasn't going to work and heading to Georgia Southern to get his master's degree and serving as the pitching coach. From there, he returned to Florida and after three years at the high school level, he was able to come back to Stetson as an assistant.

Just three years later, at age 30, he ascended to become the school's head coach in the summer of 1979. He stayed there through the 2016 season (serving as "head coach emeritus" in 2017), some 37 years and more than 1,300 wins later.

Running through Dunn's CV just shows that the guy knew a little something about the college game and how to recruit players. While the state of Florida typically is brimming with outstanding talent, it can be tough when competing with the University of Floridas and Miamis of the world. But he liked deGrom's athleticism, entirely as an infielder, having seen him at his small high school and in summer American Legion action while playing for DeLand Post 6, enough to bring him to campus.

"It was always my philosophy to try to recruit the really good quality Division I local kids and we were fortunate here being in Central Florida that we did have quite a few," Dunn said. "Obviously, Jacob fit that mold. We had seen him as a shortstop and left-handed hitter, and he just kind of fit what we were looking for.

"He was an outstanding shortstop. Yeah, he was lanky—and that's to put it mildly—but he had tremendous hands for some-body that was tall, had very good range. And of course, the arm speaks for itself."

If deGrom ever pitched in high school, neither Dunn nor his staff ever saw him. It was the infield all the way. And that's where he played throughout his freshman year, though his first college action came at third base in deference to All-Conference shortstop Casey Frawley, who went on to be a 17th-round draft pick of the Cleveland Indians in 2009 (a year where he moved to play second and the outfield to make room for deGrom's supe-rior defensive ability). In a sign of what was to come offensively, deGrom hit .243 and slugged .271 over 107 at-bats as freshman, picking up just three extra-base hits—all doubles—along the way.

He was the Hatters' everyday shortstop in 2009, once again showing excellent actions and a plus arm from the premium posi-tion while compiling a modest .258/.296/.289 line, this time with four doubles in the extra-base hit column in 128 at-bats. Some progress, but he wasn't exactly being invited to play short in the Cape Cod League or for Team USA. Still, Dunn has pondered whether that route would have borne professional fruit.

"A lot of people ask me if he would have made it as a shortstop and I tell them, 'I really do, seeing the progress he made going into his junior year.' I think that he would have had an opportunity to sign maybe as a low draft pick as a shortstop because of his range and his arm and being a left- handed hitter," Dunn said. "Everyone says, 'Would he have achieved the success that he's had with the Mets?' And I said, 'I'm not that smart of a guy.' If I was a betting man, I would've said no. But I think he would have had an opportunity to play some pro ball as a shortstop. Where it went from there, I can't tell you."

May 6, 2009. That's the moment where everything started to change for deGrom, though on the surface it looks like nothing more than a random mid-week game against the University of Central Florida. It's one the Hatters would likely rather forget overall, an ugly 14–9 loss. But at the end of that game, their shortstop popped on the mound for some mop-up duty. One inning, six pitches, five strikes, two groundball outs, and one strikeout. Jacob deGrom the pitcher was born.

———

That one inning of work planted a seed with Dunn and the rest of the Stetson coaching staff, who began brewing up an idea that deGrom could serve as the school's closer while still playing shortstop regularly. This is not a revolutionary idea in the college game. Huston Street played third base for the University of Texas and would warm up by throwing with someone on the sidelines in between batters if he had to, all before going on to saving 324 big league games. Matt Wieters was Georgia Tech's catcher and closer before becoming the No. 5 overall pick in the 2007 Draft as a backstop and spending a dozen years behind the plate in the major leagues.

What deGrom didn't have, however, was experience. In some ways, the fact deGrom was not considered elite enough to garner a Cape Cod League invite may have worked to his advantage. Instead, deGrom had the opportunity to stay at home, at Stetson's home park, to play for the DeLand Suns in the Florida Collegiate Summer League.

The Suns had joined the league as an expansion team in 2008 and moved from Orlando to DeLand in 2009 with former big league All-Star and World Series-winning manager Davey Johnson as the head coach.

Johnson, of course, won the 1986 World Series with the Mets and skippered the Reds, Orioles, Dodgers and Nationals after that. In 2009, he was two years shy of taking that job in Washington. While deGrom still wanted to play up the middle, Dunn reached out to him about trying to find some innings for him to see how it looked. The original thought was that deGrom would get to do both, which is what Dunn envisioned for him for the 2010 season.

His first outing came on June 6, 2009, entering the game with runners on first and second and two outs. deGrom, with all of one inning of pitching experience under his belt, calmly got a strikeout and a ground out to end the threat. He appeared in a total of five games, all in relief, between June 6 and June 20. He picked up two wins and amassed 6⅓ innings, allowing one unearned run on six hits and just one walk while striking out six.

But that was it, and not because of some agreed upon innings limit. Johnson would've loved to have used him more on a team that finished the FCSL regular season with the best record, with a roster that included future big leaguers like Peter O'Brien (then a catcher), outfielder Jabari Blash, and pitcher Jimmy Nelson. But deGrom took his glove and went home (it wasn't far after all) because it was not an either/or proposition for him, it was both/and. He was a shortstop willing to throw some, but there was no playing time for him in the infield that summer. In fact, his at-bats equaled the amount of earned runs he gave up: zero. After a few weeks and those five outings, he saw the writing on the wall and called it a summer.

"I went to that summer ball team as a pitcher and didn't know why," deGrom told the *New York Post* in 2014. "I spoke to the coaches and said, 'I don't think I'm pitching in college.' Nobody had told me, so I kind of talked to the coach and it didn't work out. I stopped playing so I could hit and because I wasn't getting any practice doing what I thought I'd be doing in college."

"I couldn't get him at-bats," said Johnson, recalling he had another shortstop taking up most of the time at that spot that summer. "I felt bad that I couldn't accommodate him. He's the only guy in my career that ever didn't come back. He didn't want to pitch for me, for his reasons.

"I didn't hold it against him. I was the same kind of person. If you didn't agree with me, trade me or get rid of me. I understood where he was coming from. That was his choice and I admired that. It wasn't that he didn't want to pitch. He wanted to hit. I don't blame him for that. At the time, I wish he had talked to me more. But it hasn't turned out too bad for him."

It was a small sample, sure, but Johnson knew right away deGrom had a special arm, claiming it takes five minutes for someone who truly understands the game to ascertain if a player has any ability. And between deGrom's live arm and his ability to instantaneously fill up the strike zone, Johnson knew that there was something there. To Johnson, he passed his Satchel Paige test. Let's let Johnson explain:

I faced Satchel Paige. After the game, I went up to him and said, 'Satch, you're a great pitcher, what's your best pitch?' He said, 'It's my B pitch.' I asked, 'What in the fuck is a B pitch?' His response: 'It be what I want it to be.' From that point, anytime I saw a pitcher who could throw the ball where they wanted to, in, out, up, down—whether it was Dwight Gooden or Jacob deGrom—he was a Satchel Paige guy.

He could locate. Aside from that, he had a great arm. I was a little upset he left. He could flat out pitch. It doesn't take a rocket scientist to understand talent. You never know what's going to happen to players, but when he left the squad, I was really disappointed. He has a great arm. That attitude didn't hurt him. It helped get him to where he is now.

I probably should've played him like Ohtani, pitched him and played him at short. Tell him I'm sorry, I fucked up on that deal.

———

The unofficial fall season in college baseball is a time for players to get some work in, try some new things out and largely lay the groundwork for the upcoming spring. And one thing Dunn and his staff wanted deGrom to work on was pitching. They knew they would have to broach the subject carefully, given his summer ball experience. The last thing they wanted to do was turn him off of the idea completely or, even worse, have him walk away from the program like he did the DeLand Suns.

"He loved shortstop, he did not want to pitch full-time; he wanted to play short," Dunn said. "But we talked to him."

The plan was simple: Play shortstop on a regular basis and serve as the team's closer, bringing him in for the eighth or ninth inning when the team had a lead. It wouldn't be a heavy workload and because he had (and has) such a clean arm action, there was confidence he could be back at short the next day.

"That was somewhat appealing to him," Dunn said. "He said, 'Yeah, it sounds good to me.'"

So, deGrom spent the fall before his junior year as Stetson's closer and got plenty of mound time, while also continuing to take batting practice and get ground balls as a shortstop. Pitching was still very much secondary on his mind, at best, but he showed that innate ability to throw strikes regardless of how little work he did in bullpen sessions. He exhibited outstanding command of his fastball to go along with a nice little slider and even a changeup; remarkable, Dunn remembers, given that he hadn't, and wasn't, logging much time with a pitching coach.

He also wasn't seen all that much. The fall is a time when scouts build their lists of players, a preference or follow list, helping them prioritize who they want to see when the spring season begins. There are a limited number of days in the fall to see players, with most colleges having perhaps one official scout day to go along with a small smattering of exhibitions or intrasquad games. In that area of Florida, a scout might try to hit multiple locations in one fall day.

The odds, then, of a scout sticking around until late in an afternoon to see a light-hitting shortstop work as a late-inning reliever were slim. And even if they did, the 88–91 mph deGrom was topping out at during that time would not have turned many heads. But all it takes is one scout to see something new, to notice something others weren't around to see, to change the course of a young player's career.

That one scout was Les Parker, then an area scout with the New York Mets. And if it hadn't been for a string of random events and professional connections, Parker may have never been in DeLand that fall at all.

Parker had been a high school standout in the Tampa area who signed with the Dodgers after being taken in the 1966 Draft. His minor league career didn't amount to much after he hurt his knees playing basketball during the offseason, back at a time when major league teams didn't monitor their players' activities as closely. After Parker walked away from playing in 1969, he figured he was done with the game of baseball. He and—by the scouting butterfly effect, if you will—Jacob deGrom, has George Steinbrenner's daughter to thank for his career.

Parker was happily teaching and coaching basketball at St. Lawrence Catholic School when his fellow coach, Joe Molloy, married Jessica Steinbrenner and left to work in the family business: the New York Yankees. Parker was reluctant initially, not interested in the travel that often accompanies life in the game, but eventually relented and joined his former coach two years later. Molloy would go on to be a managing partner of the organization and helped run the team when George Steinbrenner was suspended in the early 1990s.

Parker spent 11 years with the organization, learning from legendary executives like George Bradley and Gene Michael along the way. From there, he worked as a major league scout for the Texas Rangers for three years and then to the Cincinnati Reds for three more. Figuring he'd had as long of a run as he was going to have, he went back to "civilian life" as a teacher, at least until one of his colleagues from the Texas Rangers, Rudy Terrasas, called him up, offering him a job. Terrasas had been hired to be the scouting director for the Mets ahead of the 2006 Draft and he wanted Parker to join his staff.

"I said, 'No, I'm not interested. I'm teaching again. I'm at a school that I really like. You don't really need me,'" Parker recalls telling Terrasas initially.

Terrasas obviously convinced Parker to rejoin the scouting world and that fall of 2009 was right in the middle of a five-year run as a full-time area scout for the Mets organization before continuing part-time in Florida for the next decade.

Stetson University was a regular stopping point for scouts in the area and Parker was familiar with deGrom's work as a shortstop. He actually had some early interest when he saw him during his freshman and sophomore years because of his athleticism and, of course, his arm strength. But that waned when Parker felt that deGrom might not hit enough, especially from a power standpoint, to be a position player at the next level.

Parker was at a scout day in DeLand that day when deGrom came in for one of his late-in-the-day outings. Scouts often head to these events hoping to uncover a gem, though it's typically more useful to add more information to already-known college players. By the time deGrom came in, Parker estimates that of the 25 scouts who were in attendance at the start of the day, perhaps only a half-dozen remained to watch deGrom throw a ton of strikes while hitting the low-90s at best in his one inning of work. If anyone else was excited, they didn't let on. But Parker got on the phone immediately, calling regional cross-checker Steve Barningham.

"I called Barney and said, 'I found a player today,'" Parker recalled.

Barney retorted by telling Parker he thought he was just going to see Stetson, a school with no known top draft prospects at the time. Parker chuckled and confirmed that's where he went. Barningham was even more surprised when his area scout told him the player he was referring to was Jacob deGrom.

"He said, 'Last you told me, Jacob deGrom couldn't hit.' I said, 'Well, he can't hit, but he sure can pitch.'"

Parker gleaned that from a one-inning look, relying on the type of pitcher the Mets coveted at the time, as well as the lessons taught to him by past mentors.

"We profile pitchers, obviously, like everybody else," Parker said. "And our profile, he fit it perfectly: wide shoulders, narrow hips, long arms, easy actions. Gene Michael was one of my early mentors and he used to tell me to just look for guys who do it easy. And boy, he did it easy. He was 92 and he hadn't pitched before. Now I'm not smart enough to say that he was going to throw 97. But he was easy 92. And what impressed me was he spun the ball well, and he did not throw one pitch above the waist. And it was like a classic delivery. So I was convinced right away. That's how it all started. I just happened to run into him."

But Parker wouldn't have the ability to continue scouting deGrom, much to his chagrin. The Mets' scouting personnel shifted around in the Sunshine state and Parker had to focus on a different part of the state. At first, he wanted to keep Stetson on his plate, largely because of deGrom, but relented and handed his find over to Steve Nichols.

Nichols, for his part, was no neophyte in the game. Baseball was handed down from one generation to the next in the Nichols family. Steve's grandfather, Chet, was a right-hander who spent parts of six seasons pitching in the big leagues in the late 1920s and early 1930s. His father, also named Chet, was a lefty who logged nine seasons in the major leagues, playing with Hall of Famers Eddie Mathews and Warren Spahn.

While Bumpy, Nichols' nickname among scouts, was given the love of baseball from two generations of Nichols men, he did not inherit the talent gene, a self-described "good field, no hit" infielder who never got a real opportunity to play. And you know what they say, those who can't do, teach. Or in the case of baseball. Those who can't play, coach.

He coached college baseball for a dozen years, with stops at Georgia Southern, Florida Southern, and the University of Florida before he entered the world of scouting, starting with the Oakland A's back in 1989. After seven years with the A's, he logged three with the San Diego Padres and spent a decade with the Detroit Tigers. That led to the two years with the Mets central to this story before he spent seven with the White Sox. For those scoring at home, that's approximately four decades in the game.

He also lived almost within spitting distance of Stetson when he was hired by the Mets, so the handoff made a lot of sense. But Parker got one guarantee from Barningham before letting go.

"My agreement with Barney was very simple," Parker said. "I said, 'Barney. I'll let him have Stetson, but only if you promise to go see deGrom, no matter what Bumpy says.' And I trusted Bumpy, though I didn't know him as well then as I do now—a great scout and great guy and good friend. But Bumpy saw the same thing. And the rest is history."

Now it's not like Parker got a sworn affidavit that deGrom would get seen, let alone drafted. Nichols, Barningham would have to sign off, not to mention Terrasas, the scouting director who brought Parker to the Mets, and even general manager Omar Minaya.

Nichols was about 30 years into his baseball life the year deGrom would get drafted, in 2010, and it didn't take long for him to see the upside in the inexperienced right-hander's arm. And to tell him he wasn't going to pass muster as a short-stop, not that deGrom wanted to hear any of it the first time they met. The exchange went something like this, according to Nichols' memory of the meeting and told with the remnants of a New England accent that gives away his Rhode Island upbringing:

> Nichols: You know, I've got no interest in you as an infielder.
> deGrom: Geez, I think I can hit. I know they say I'm not a good hitter, but I can hit. I think I can play professional baseball and be a shortstop and hit.

When deGrom broke out of the gate getting a few hits here and there, Nichols did have a minute of thinking maybe the kid was right, but he regressed to the mean and went 7-for-31 (.226) through the first several games in February that season. Meanwhile, he tossed 1⅔ hitless innings, striking out four and getting the save in his first appearance as the team's closer and he didn't give up a hit until his fourth outing.

Nichols, who did see him throw in the fall, didn't see any of that. He was busy getting first spring looks at the high school talent in the area, putting deGrom and Stetson on the back burner, letting him log some innings before checking in on his progress. That was his plan, at least, until Dunn called up his old friend to chastise him for not having stopped by, a baseball veteran's version of "You don't call, you don't write!"

"He said, 'Where you been? You haven't been in to see deGrom. All your buddies and everybody have been in here,'" Nichols recounted. "And I said, 'Why do I want to run in there quick and see a shortstop throw one inning? That does nothing for me.' There was silence on the phone. 'When he starts to throw extended innings, I want an extended look.' He says, 'Funny you should say that. I'm throwing him [this weekend]. And he's going to start.'"

Getting deGrom to a yes on that move was, as you might imagine, easier said than done. He had signed off on closing while still playing shortstop and had done well with it, tossing 5⅔ scoreless with just one hit and no walks allowed, striking out six and picking up two saves. But Stetson's starting rotation had faltered to start the year, struggling with the first game of the weekend series in particular.

Friday night is typically when the ace of a college staff starts. Stephen Strasburg pitched on Fridays for San Diego State before he was the No. 1 pick in the 2009 Draft. Justin Verlander was Old Dominion's Friday night starter in 2004, the year he was the

No. 2 overall pick. The 2010 college season featured Friday start-
ers like Matt Harvey (the No. 7 overall pick in that June's draft)
at North Carolina and Chris Sale, the No. 13 overall pick from
Florida Gulf Coast University (more on him later). Stetson had
gone 0–3 over the first three Fridays of the 2010 season, losing
by a combined score of 34–12. Dunn knew a change needed to
be made and he had a feeling the guy he wanted wasn't going
to be too thrilled about it.

"We were not even close to being real competitive on that
key Friday night game of the three-game series," Dunn said. "We
were about 13–14 games into the year and I think he had two
saves, so our best arm was wasting away in Margaritaville out
there and at shortstop.

"I call the staff and I said guys, 'You're going to think I'm
crazy, but I think we need to consider talking to Jacob and see
if we can move him into Friday night.' My pitching coach, he
was pretty supportive. My infield guy thought I had one eye in
the middle of my forehead and he was not for it at all."

The hesitation came because deGrom did add such defensive
value at shortstop, but Dunn's rationale was that you had to be
in games for that to matter and this was their best way to be
more competitive. He took what was assuredly more than a few
deep breaths before presenting his plan to his shortstop/closer,
the one who had walked out on Davey Johnson for wanting him
to only pitch that summer.

"He may have been a little more receptive to it than what he
was with Davey, but he wasn't he wasn't real enthusiastic," Dunn
said. "But he was a team guy. He said, 'Let me ask you this. I
move into a starting role, can I still play short?'"

If this were the movie version of the Jacob deGrom story,
perhaps there would be some dramatic music to signify the
moment when his career really changed course. Dunn had to
lay out that it would be different than when he was pitching

in relief. He couldn't start on a Friday and then play shortstop the next day or his arm would fall off. It would take some figuring out, but Dunn did make some assurances that deGrom would get to play some shortstop and swing the bat a little as they moved forward.

"He reluctantly said, 'Well, if that's what it's going to take, if you think we have a better chance to win, I'm in.' So that's kind of a long story of how that transition took place."

deGrom's first start actually came on a Saturday, March 13, though it was the opener of a three-game series against Old Dominion. His final line that afternoon was nothing to write home about—five innings, six hits, four earned runs, one walk, and two strikeouts—but keep in mind it was the first start he had ever made, and it was the first time he was stretching beyond one or two innings of relief work.

At this point of the spring, most other scouts had gone on to focus on the always-deep high school class in Florida. And while deGrom had been successful out of the bullpen, his 88–91 mph fastball certainly didn't make the scouts who might have seen him early sit up and take notice.

But Bump Nichols was sure he was there. One thing a good evaluator does is to scout the scouts. It's always good to know who else is seeing what you're seeing, and Nichols surveyed the ballpark and realized there wasn't much action, with just two or three other scouts in attendance. One was Tim Rock, then with the San Francisco Giants, worth noting because he (and his team) would be the one Nichols (and the Mets) would worry about the most when it came time to deciding when and if to draft deGrom.

"Every time I turned around, Tim Rock was there when I was there," said Nichols, who remembers seeing deGrom pitch five or six times the rest of the spring. "And a lot of times we were the only two guys there."

That first start, deGrom was, well, what he'd been during his briefer stints on the mound: a steady strike-throwing machine who didn't light up a radar gun.

"He was 88–91, maybe he bumped a 92 in the first inning," Nichols said. "He had this little cutter they were trying to get him to do stuff with and he had a feel for a change. It wasn't a great one, but there was always some action to it. And you said, 'Man, this this guy's arm works good.'"

Nichols particularly liked how deGrom, even when he warmed up, would start from the bottom of the strike zone and work his way up. It's not that he never missed up, but he seemed to understand from the get-go that it was much easier to limit damage down than up in the zone.

"He just kind of went about his business, working from the bottom up," Nichols said. "Miss downstairs and come in maybe eight inches into the strike zone, rather than a missing up and coming three feet down through the hitting zone type of thing. And that's kind of how he was."

For his part, Rock saw exactly the same thing as Nichols and felt that his scouting colleague was as ubiquitous as Nichols felt Rock was. Rock was a longtime scout who was only a part-timer for the Giants at the time. Because he wasn't in charge of an entire area, he could focus on a smaller handful of players. He was a Pepperidge Farm distributor by day and a scout by afternoon and night, explaining that the baked goods gig afforded him the time to spend all afternoon/evening evaluating players.

He was one of the few who saw deGrom more than once as a reliever because he was taught never to leave a game early, so he was able to see the right-hander in his brief stint as Stetson closer, then saw the transition to the head of the rotation, thinking he'd be flying solo at that first start against Old Dominion.

"I thought I was the only one that was going to see it that night because there was another player that was a high profile guy I thought other guys were going to go take a look at," said Rock, who now helps run the Florida Travel Baseball team, a program who has seen players like Francisco Lindor, Javy Baez, and Jesse Winker come through its doors, and is the creator of iProScoutBaseball Systems. "The way it's situated at Stetson, where the stadium is, you walk out… I walked out and I thought, 'Oh I'm the only one here.' I looked down and right below me was Bumpy. And I thought, 'Damn it.'"

Rock knew the draft order in 2010. The Mets had the seventh pick in each round; the Giants picked 23rd. He knew that if the Mets were on deGrom, they'd be able to get him in any given round ahead of his team. He had to hope, then, that his reports would lead to the Giants liking deGrom more than the Mets did. And he did like what he saw.

"The thing that I liked about him was his delivery was so free and easy," Rock said. "And he had great extension, and he had movement on his pitches. You know, he's the type of guy who used to throw pitches, they're coming right over the plate, and people would swing and miss and I'm thinking, 'How does that happen?'"

Luckily for deGrom, he got to ease into being the ace. All he had to do in his second-ever start was face Florida Gulf Coast University and a tall lefty by the name of Chris Sale. deGrom held his own, stretching out to six innings, allowing three runs (two earned), striking out five and, of course, walking no one. Unfortunately for him and Stetson, Sale went eight, gave up just one run and struck out 14. Sale would go on to be the No. 13 overall pick in the 2010 Draft and through the 2022 season has accrued the second most WAR in the class. (For those of you scoring at home, deGrom is third on that list, trailing only No. 3 pick Manny Machado and Sale and landing in front of No. 1 selection Bryce Harper.)

Stetson and FGCU are in the same conference, so this would not be the only time the two future All-Stars would meet as the two would square off in the conference tournament at the end of the collegiate season. As frequently as Nichols and Rock were in watching deGrom, those were two starts they didn't attend. Knowing Sale would bring in a lot of scouts, including cross-checkers, scouting directors and maybe even some general managers, they knew their guy would get seen by others in their respective organizations, so they could go and check on other players.

The Mets crosschecker, Barningham, had already seen him pitch before that first matchup against Sale. A former minor leaguer who got his start in scouting with the Oakland A's, Barningham joined the Mets in December 2005 as an area scout covering North Florida. He was no stranger to finding late-round talent as the area scout responsible for Daniel Murphy becoming a Met courtesy of a 13th-round selection in 2006. He got bumped up to be the East Coast crosschecker in 2008, so 2010 was just his third Draft in the supervisory gig. It was an enormous amount of the country to oversee, so much so the Mets split it up into separate Southeast and Northeast jobs, in 2011. But in 2010, Barningham had to try to get everywhere, from Maine down to his home in the Sunshine State.

Needless to say, he didn't get to Florida as much as he would have liked. Luckily for him and the Mets, with Parker and Nichols still in their employ, Barningham knew he had six decades of baseball experience to rely on.

"You really had to rely on your area scouts, they had to be good," said Barningham, who is now the Mets' director of international scouting. "And I had two guys with 30 years of experience apiece, which made my life pretty easy. I could leave home and I knew it was safe. I knew those guys had it on lock. Steve Nichols and Les Parker were amazing for me because I was still young. I was like 35 years old, still trying to figure it out."

One thing he figured out early is when you make a promise to someone with the experience of a Les Parker, you make sure you fulfill it. So Barningham made sure to get an early look at deGrom, even before Dunn inserted him into the Stetson rotation. Now, any crosschecker worth anything isn't going to sit on a college team for multiple days just to see a short-stop-turned-reliever who is just bumping 90 mph on the radar gun. No, Barningham looked at Stetson's schedule and saw that the Hatters were traveling to the University of Georgia for just their second series of the 2010 season.

That year, the Georgia Bulldogs had a number of legitimate pitching prospects, starting with Justin Grimm, a right-hander who would eventually go in the fifth round to the Rangers and spend parts of eight years in the big leagues. He'd be one of five Georgia pitchers to get drafted in June that year, a group that included Mets seventh-rounder Jeff Walters, further proof that Barningham had a very productive weekend in Athens in late February, though it wasn't easy.

"Georgia had real arms that year so you could sit at Georgia and hopefully see deGrom pitch," Barningham said. "It was the last week of February and it was about 37 degrees. And it was miserable. I grinded it out."

At this point, deGrom's college pitching résumé consisted of two games and two total innings, hitless as they may have been. Georgia routed Stetson on Friday, 12–2, and won again on Saturday. Finally, on Sunday, with the Hatters down 7–4, Barningham finally got to see deGrom in action, as he tossed another perfect frame with one strikeout in the eighth inning of an eventual 7–5 Stetson loss.

"He went 1-for-4 at the plate and they let him pitch the last inning," Barningham recalled. "And it was for real. He might have touched 92. It wasn't firm, but he moved the right way. The ball was super tight."

Barningham looked around and thought there wasn't another scout in sight, not surprising given that it was the final inning of a Sunday game. He thought he could keep deGrom a secret...

until he saw Major League Baseball Scouting Bureau video technician Christie Stancil Wood (who, if you ask anyone in baseball, seemed to be at every single East Coast game) leaving the ballpark.

"Most everybody had left," Wood recalled. "It was me, Barney, and one other scout—Paul Turco with the Giants—still there. I had mostly put the camera away. I saw him come in to pitch and thought, 'Hey that's that shortstop. I need to see what he can do.'

"I started coming down the steps and Barney and Turk starts asking me what I'm doing. 'I'm checking him out.' They're like, 'But you don't have him turned in.' But everyone knows my work ethic; I wanted to see what he could do. There was just something about him, he was loose and easy. I got him on film pitching and turned him in. Everyone knew that once I saw him, the word would be out [because MLSB video was shared with all 30 clubs]. Barney told me to not send in the film. He and I still talk about it when we see each other."

"I remember walking out with her and I was like, 'You have to sit on that video. You can't turn that in,'" Barningham said. "At that point, it was so early, I thought I might be the only guy who gets to see this guy, at least a supervisor. So I was pretty ecstatic about it. We kind of felt like we were hiding him out. And then they started him against Chris Sale. And that ship sailed pretty quick."

While he did spend the rest of the spring as Stetson's No. 1 starter, the Mets' desire to keep deGrom stashed away was helped by the fact he wasn't blowing people away, both in terms of radar-gun readings and the numbers he was putting up. He did manage to go fairly deep into starts more often than not, keeping Stetson in games, but between the two Sale matchups, he had a 4.52 ERA and allowed more than 12 hits per nine (though he continued to be stingy with walks at 2.11 per nine) over nine starts.

The last start before facing Sale in the Atlantic Sun Conference Tournament was his best. He pitched into the 10th, allowing just one run on five hits, walking two and striking out nine, a career high. He threw 128 pitches and then had to throw on five days rest—keep in mind that it was usually seven days rest between starts during the year—in the opener of the tournament in Nashville.

In the sequel against Sale, deGrom was okay, not great, allowing five runs on seven hits over six innings. Of course, he walked only one. Sale gave up six hits and two runs over seven innings, striking out 11. Conference tournaments are typically the last look the higher-ups in scouting departments get before the draft; area scouts might go cover the NCAA Regionals the following week, but crosscheckers and scouting directors are usually in their draft rooms lining up their boards by then.

For both pitchers, that was the last look, period. Neither Stetson nor FGCU made into Regional play, with the Hatters losing to Sale and the Eagles and then to Jacksonville. Florida Gulf Coast lost its next two after beating deGrom and Stetson and that was that. In many ways, the biggest memory from the Sale-deGrom matchup was that deGrom hit his one and only collegiate home run against Sale in the second inning of the game. It was, perhaps, a sign of things to come as while deGrom may not have been able to hit enough to make it as a shortstop, he proved to be a very good hitting pitcher in the National League, with three career homers through 2021.

————

By the time the 2010 Draft rolled around, there weren't that many teams who really coveted deGrom the way the Mets scouts did, even if they feared the matchup against Sale in front of so many other evaluators would let their secret out of the bag. But as someone who wasn't a high-priority player, he wasn't seen by everyone in the front office. Terrasas, the scouting director who had brought Parker over from the Rangers and had also hired

Nichols, never saw deGrom pitch in person before the draft. That's not uncommon for later-round picks, with only so many days in a spring for a director to go out and see players. There was the possibility Terrasas could have seen him had he gone to see Sale pitch in that tournament game, but the Mets' scouting director wasn't really on Sale, who scared several teams off because of what was thought to be an unorthodox delivery and arm slot that could lead to injury.

Luckily for the Mets, the triumvirate of Parker, Nichols, and Barningham all had him firmly on their collective radar, while others both in the room and out might have been focusing elsewhere.

The Mets picked No. 7 overall that year and picking high up in the first round does carry some extra pressure to get it right, not that it always happens that way. Add in the fact that the Mets didn't have a true first round pick in 2006, 2007 or 2009, forfeiting them as a result of signing big league free agents, there was a lot of attention on what the Mets would do at the very top. The target ended up being a different pitcher, Matt Harvey, from the University of North Carolina, who was one of the top college arms in the entire class.

"When you're general manager of the New York Mets, you don't have as much time as you would like to get out there and scout guys," said Omar Minaya, the Mets' GM from 2004 to 2010. "I did see Harvey and I did see a list of guys because we were picking seventh. I was out more that year than other years. Now, that being said, I did not hear about deGrom's name up until when the team came to the draft room and we started talking about him.

"I still remember the conversation. It was a fall look [the one Parker had] that stayed in people's minds. And it was all about, to me, the physical athleticism. To this day, it's hard for me to pass up good athletes. It's a philosophy."

Every year, Terrasas would invite a number of area scouts, along with his crosscheckers, into the draft room. In 2010, both Nichols and Parker were on the invite list, so the two area guys who liked deGrom the most were with Barningham in "the room where it happens."

"We set up a big board of the top 100 [overall talent in the draft]," said Terrasas, who still works for the Mets in professional scouting. "And then with the remaining players, what we do is we rank them by position. So usually, when that big board comes off, you've probably eaten up about five, maybe six rounds. So after that big board unravels, the scouts that are in the room, they start campaigning for their players. They start chirping, and I first started hearing the guys that actually laid eyes on Jacob, starting around the sixth round."

"Before the end of the spring came around, I said to Barney, 'You know, this guy probably should be a fourth or fifth round guy,'" Nichols said. "I said, 'When it's all said and done, that's probably what he's going to end up being.' And he said, 'He's gotten better,' but he then still ended up lasting until the ninth. I don't think anybody was too far off."

While things started to get tense for some deGrom supporters right around that sixth round, Parker wasn't overly concerned about it. It helped he hadn't seen deGrom since that look in the fall and had his own area to focus on. So when the Mets finally took him with pick No. 272 in the 2010 Draft, he felt that was about right.

"I was 'Whoop, whoop!' I'll tell you that," Parker said. "I really was happy that we got him. But I didn't realize that he had matched up against Sale. If I would've known that, I probably would have thought he'd go earlier."

Rock was not in the Giants' draft room that day, so he couldn't start chirping at his director, but he knew there was some interest in deGrom. He even thought there was some consideration of taking him in the sixth round. Instead, San Francisco took Mike Kickham, a lefty out of Missouri State, who has made it to the big leagues.

That's right around where Barningham thought the first opportunity to take deGrom would come, the spot where he thought the draft would "start getting soft," and where the Mets could take advantage of having a lot more history on him than other teams, who even if they were intrigued from the Sale matchup, would not have seen him pitch as much as the Mets did.

"That's where I was like, 'We have to make a move,'" Barningham said. "This is the one guy we don't want to lose. And so when the draft starts getting to a point where they all start kind of sounding the same, that's where you say, 'Hey, I'll make sure I'm getting my guy. I'm not leaving here without my guy.' You have to be in that room to get a feel for the premium part of [that particular] draft, [and if it's] starting to decline. So that's where you start to push for the guys that you gotta have. And that was a guy we felt like we had to have."

In the sixth round, the Mets took Greg Peavey, a right-hander from Oregon State. Round 7 is when the Mets took Jeff Walters, that Georgia right-hander Barningham saw that weekend way back in February. In the eighth round, they went the junior college route by selecting another right-handed pitcher, Kenny McDowall from College of Southern Nevada. As each chance to take deGrom went by, the trio undoubtedly felt uneasy, led by a stressed-out Barney.

"I was probably having a heart attack," Barningham joked. "Each round, you're thinking, 'Oh my gosh.' We had a point where finally they're like, 'Hey, we're taking him next, calm down.' And then we took somebody else. And that's when we were thinking, 'What's going on? He's not going to be around.' The three of us, we identified that this was our guy. And it's easy to look back now. And I think every draft, you have a couple names like that are 'my guys.' But we got him. And I think we were more relieved than anything."

"I truly believe in the scouts and I was fortunate enough that I listened to them," Terrasas said. "Because if you look back, Jacob was strictly a scout selection. Because if you look at the numbers, they weren't very attractive. But both these guys in Florida, as well as our crosschecker, they understood what we were hunting. And Jacob checked off so many of the boxes that we were looking for, from athleticism, the height, we loved the delivery, it was repeatable, we loved the arm action, it was clean. We loved his competitiveness.

"His stuff wasn't what it is today, but it was projectable. We thought that it was a guy, or at least they were telling me it was a guy that didn't have a lot of innings, so it was pretty much a fresh arm. And we felt like there was upside. So when we got to that ninth round, thank God I listened. You know that old saying you'd rather be lucky than good? That's exactly what happened here, I'll be quite honest with you. Because if I would have known he would have turned out to be what he is today, he would have been the first pick in 2010 or shortly thereafter."

———

The improbable story of Jacob deGrom as the best pitcher in the National League didn't end there. He pitched briefly that summer in the rookie-level Appalachian League before blowing out his elbow and needing Tommy John surgery. That caused him to miss all of 2011, forcing him even further off the radar screens of even the most die-hard prospect fanatics. But a funny thing happened to Jacob deGrom the way to complete obscurity: He worked his ass off while rehabbing from elbow surgery. When he re-emerged in 2012 with the Mets' Low-A affiliate in the South

Atlantic League, he started to look a lot more like the dominant starter with unhittable stuff than the super-athletic infielder
who could throw strikes. It didn't take long for reports to start
coming in. Even Minaya, who was let go by the Mets after the
2010 season and was working with the Padres, heard about it.

"Two springs later, I'm hearing, 'Hey Omar, that guy deGrom,
he's blowing,'" Minaya said. "A lot of the guys still work there
and they start telling me about deGrom, 'This guy is lights out;
you have to go see him!'"

In the spring of 2012, Barningham was already neck-deep in
crosschecking that year's draft class, so he was not exactly honing
in on what was going on at the lower levels of the Mets' system.
But he didn't have to.

"My phone started ringing, pro scouts were calling me and
asking, 'Who is this guy?'" Barningham said. "That's when I knew
something was up. One scout called me and said he's getting 98
pretty easy. I was like, 'Come on!'

"That's when I thought, 'Oh boy!' because I knew he was
going to throw strikes. But when that velocity came, it was like
'Holy cow!' You knew for sure he was pitching in the big leagues."

During that 2012 season, Nichols got a call from the son
of an old scouting friend, a scout himself who had moved from
the amateur to the pro side, telling him in breathless tones
about an arm he saw in Savannah, the Mets' South Atlantic
League affiliate.

"He said, 'Boy did I see a guy throw last night,'" Nichols
recalled. "I asked if he was any good. And he said, 'Yeah. The
guy came out and threw about eight innings and, man, he was
95–98. He struck out about eight and walked one.' And then
he said it was deGrom.

"I said, 'He's throwing that hard?' I didn't realize he was
throwing that hard. Now you start thinking, 'What did I write
on that report?'"

It's to deGrom's, and the Mets player development staff's, credit that he went from the guy on that report throwing 91–92 mph, tops, with a tiny little cutter-like slider, to the guy who would win awards, go to All-Star Games and generally make the best hitters in the sport look silly for several years. The scouts who saw some kind of future for him back in 2010 certainly won't take too much credit.

"When you saw Jacob that fall and in that early spring, it's tough to visualize that this guy is going to be a Rookie of the Year and win two Cy Young Awards," Nichols said. "I enjoy it and I enjoy watching him and I do say to myself, 'Nice job.' But I don't turn around and pat myself on the back. I've got a bad shoulder and it doesn't get that far around anymore."

Chapter 4

Mookie Betts

The **2011 Draft** is likely going to go down as one of the greatest of all time since the draft was instituted in 1965.

It's a bit too early to tell for sure, since so many from that class are in the primes of their careers as of this writing. Whether it lives up to 1985, generally considered to be the standard bearer, we'll have to wait and see, but it belongs in the conversation.

The very top of the draft was very, very good and has lived up to that billing. The college crop that year produced No. 1 overall pick Gerrit Cole, No. 6 pick Anthony Rendon and No. 11 overall George Springer, among others, who have collected multiple All-Star selections and other accolades, all of whom who had WARs over 30 through the 2022 season.

The high school side is equally impressive. This is the class, after all, that sent Francisco Lindor and Javier Baez on their way, both top 10 picks. The late Jose Fernandez went in the middle of the round and Trevor Story has exceeded expectations as a supplemental first-round pick.

But the best player from this extraordinary class was not a first rounder. He went in Round 5. In 2011, my employer, MLB. com, wasn't doing draft rankings yet. *Baseball America* was the most trusted source at the time, and the leader in career WAR from this class wasn't in their Top 200 that year. Perfect Game, a leader in elite-level high school events and showcases, had him at No. 304 nationally. He wasn't even the best player in Tennessee, according to PG. He came in at No. 4.

Mookie Betts was a raw high schooler from Nashville, Tennessee, who was undersized at 5'10", 165 pounds. Most teams missed him completely. He thought he might go in the second round and when that didn't happen, he "lost interest in the draft at that point."

Luckily for him and MLB, the Boston Red Sox did not. Just how did a small, skinny high schooler from an Overton High School, a public school program that had produced a couple of big leaguers, but none since the 1983 Draft, turn into the best player in the class after going in the fifth round? It's a combination of good old-fashioned scouting and some new-fangled approaches the Red Sox were using at the time.

————

Betts was born as Markus Lynn Betts and no, it was not by design that his initials were MLB. He was named after his father, but a combination of his mother wanting to pay homage to her sister Cookie and the family being fans of the Atlanta Hawks and their point guard at the time, Mookie Blalock, led to them hanging the moniker on him at a very early age. (This must have come as a huge relief to Red Sox fans when he arrived in Boston, who had to be apoplectic about welcoming in a player potentially named after 1986 World Series nemesis Mookie Wilson.)

The fact that Betts was playing at Overton at all might have been seen as something somewhat surprising. More often than not, the young premium athletes in Nashville get snatched up by the big private schools like Montgomery Bell Academy or Brentwood

Academy. Oh, they tried, making offers to the family to have him play multiple sports at their schools.

Longtime Overton coach Mike Morrison recognized immediately that Betts had tremendous athleticism and did what he could to keep Betts' ability on the down low once he saw him playing for a local feeder program for the high school.

"There was no doubt how good of a baseball player he was," Morrison said, according to Mainstreetpreps. "I tried to keep that quiet. I didn't want for him to show up anywhere else, and we're sure appreciative that he came to Overton."

Morrison was aided by the fact that Betts' parents were believers in public education and he didn't suit up for those academies.

"My parents were the main reasons why I ended up coming to Overton," Betts said (once, again, from Mainstreetpreps). "They just didn't want to pay for [private] school and [thought] I could get my education at a public school and be very successful."

They weren't wrong, though anyone who said it was a slam dunk (something the sub six-foot Betts can do, by the way) back then is practicing some revisionist history. Yes, Betts was a very talented athlete, one who likely could have entertained offers to play college basketball and has gone on to bowl perfect games in high-level competitions. But he was small, not particularly strong, and not too many scouts thought it was going to work at the next level.

Red Sox area scout Danny Watkins was then in the minority. Watkins is a baseball lifer, one who played at Georgia Tech in the early 1980s and started coaching right after his college career was over, first as a volunteer assistant at Texas Christian University in 1983. After three years at Texas Tech (1984–86), he started the baseball program at Vernon Junior College in Texas and ran it for a decade. He spent three years as San Jacinto Junior College's pitching coach, two as a scout for the Houston Astros, made two more college coaching stops before finding what looks like his forever home with the Red Sox in October 2004 and he's been an area scout in the south with Boston since then.

It's an interesting, though not unusual path, going from coaching to scouting. Not only does Watkins look back at his time in the college ranks warmly, but he also thinks it's made him a better scout.

"We're always projecting, we're trying to figure out what a guy can be in three, four, five years and kind of understanding what it takes to make some of the adjustments needed," Watkins said. "Some adjustments are not going to be able to be made. It helped me understand the psyche of successful players, the players that came into your program, and then were successful, there were a lot of similarities between those guys. They were very driven, hard-working, they were responsible, usually the guys that performed and excelled in the classroom were the guys that were going to push themselves on the baseball field as well. So it was all those personality traits that I really enjoy seeing in some of the kids that I scout."

The first time Watkins laid eyes on Betts was the summer before his senior year of high school. File this under the "no rest for the weary" banner, but area scouts are typically out looking at the next year's talent almost immediately after the previous draft ends. It was shortly after the end of the 2010 Draft that Watkins headed to the annual Tennessee Baseball Coaches Association's showcase for rising seniors, held at Middle Tennessee State in Murfreesboro, about 35 miles southeast of Nashville.

It was a must-attend event for those who had Tennessee in their areas, with players from all over the state convening, getting split into teams, going through a workout and playing games against each other. It was Tennessee one-stop shopping for area scouts who were building follow lists—ranking players for the following year's draft class—for the next spring.

Sometimes players jump out at scouts immediately because of their physicality, how they fill out a uniform. Scouts will say "this is what they look like" or they "look the part." Betts was not one of those players in the summer of 2010.

Get used to hearing words like physicality and strength in this chapter. Because that's the number one thing that kept Betts from generating much prospect buzz. When he arrived at this showcase, his official weight might have been "soaking wet holding a brick." He's listed as 5'9", so this wasn't the kind of specimen that has an area scout calling up his bosses to rave.

But Watkins saw something in Betts right from the get-go. It wasn't how he looked, it wasn't raw power at the plate, it wasn't any one tool that screamed. It was more that everything he did was just so easy.

"The one thing that I noticed about Mook was number one, he was extremely comfortable on the field," Watkins said. "He could do just about anything without very much effort. I kind of got drawn to him, just watching how comfortable he was on the field. And he made one particular play early on in the session that kind of caught my eye and from there, I just kind of zeroed in on him a little bit more clearly."

Watkins can still describe the play vividly, as if it happened last week. Betts was at shortstop, went behind the bag, gloved the groundball, and then flipped it behind his back for a perfect toss to second base.

"He wasn't as physical as a lot of the other players there," Watkins said. "But he had that quality about him that just made me believe that this guy was someone we were going to be able to project on."

Betts had other opportunities in that summer of 2010 to impress scouts, and not just ones in Tennessee. The East Coast Professional Showcase is an event, run by major league scouts, that has taken place annually since 1996, bringing in around

150 players from across the Eastern United States each summer. In 2010, Betts was there. So was Watkins, along with area scouts, cross checkers, and scouting directors. All 30 teams have eyes and ears at East Coast Pro every year. For Watkins, it was an opportunity add to his Mookie file.

One of Betts' early strengths was his ability to move around the diamond seamlessly. At East Coast Pro, he played shortstop, second base, and center field, a precursor to what has transpired in his professional career, getting drafted as a shortstop, playing mostly second base early on, then moving to the outfield without a hitch. But Watkins wasn't a rookie. He knew that writing a report about Betts' positional flexibility, or that he would be best suited for the right side of second base, wouldn't get the higher-ups that excited.

"I just thought that in order for me to really get my message across that I felt like this was going to be a major league player, I evaluated him as a shortstop and turned him in as a shortstop, as much as there was some doubt the arm strength wasn't quite what you see today, the physicality was not there," he recalled. "But for me to turn in a high school second baseman? That would have taken a lot more convincing. So it was easier for me to keep him at shortstop and dream a little bit than it would have been to just pigeonhole him at second base. That would have been a much tougher sell."

This is more than a little sleight-of-hand a scout can employ to make sure a prospect he likes gets noticed. Did Danny Watkins believe Mookie Betts was 100 percent, no doubt about it, a long-term shortstop? No, of course not. But by turning in reports on Betts at the premium position of shortstop, it was him putting his own credentials as a scout on the line, as if to say, "This is a kid we need to seriously take a look at."

"It speaks to the scout's conviction on the total player, is what it does," Watkins said of writing a player up at one position over another, like he did with Betts. "If I can keep this guy as a shortstop in my report, make a reasonable case for that, then it speaks to the conviction that I have. You have to understand the people listening to my presentation, they want to know that I firmly believe that this guy is a major leaguer, and for me to have put him as a second baseman probably would have indicated to them less than stellar conviction."

Watkins wasn't the only one who noticed some good things about Betts that summer, of course, he just led the field headed into the turn. Perfect Game's David Rawnsley, who often scouted summer showcase events outside of his own organization's to get a feel for players in a given class, had these notes on the Tennessee prepster:

> *Plays way faster than 60 speed (6.75), impact guy on the bases, always on base, steals, takes extra base. Free swinger, fast bat, slashes and runs, contact guy, 4.19. played both OF and IF, looked most comfortable at 2B, good footwork, accurate throws, playable arm strength, quick release.*

There were other teams who turned in favorable reports and it would turn out that the San Diego Padres were probably the biggest competition, but we'll get to that in a bit. First, Mookie had to get through his other athletic endeavors before getting to the spring baseball season, his senior year in 2011.

———

Betts was a three-sport standout at Overton, but it wasn't the customary trifecta—football, basketball, baseball—we usually hear about. Yes, basketball and obviously baseball, were on his high school résumé, and the third sport may not surprise you if you've seen his exploits on the professional tour: bowling.

This wasn't just a PE class in high school, or a thing he did for fun on weekends with friends. This is a guy who bowled a perfect game in the World Series of Bowling, a rare time when a hitter wants 12 straight strikes recorded. Back at Overton, he earned Tennessee Secondary Schools Athletic Association (TSSAA) State Bowler of the Year honors in 2010. If this guy wanted to earn a living on the lanes, he could. There hasn't been too much work done on how bowling skills translate to an athlete's work on the diamond, but rest assured teams at least made note of how much Betts liked to compete and excel in anything he did.

Lest you think scouts rest up and take it easy in the winter months, Watkins, for one, made sure to go watch Betts on the basketball court, getting extra information on the athleticism and the competitiveness of the prospect. Betts was a very good basketball player, one who could have played the game collegiately had he desired, though it likely would have been at a smaller program than the University of Tennessee, where he was committed to play baseball.

Watkins also would just go and watch Betts work out, take batting practice, field grounders, as things started to move toward the 2011 season. He recalls going to see Betts play five times, over 30 competitive at-bats, over the course of that spring. His initial reports placed Betts in the fifth round, but that evolved the more he saw Betts in action.

"By the end, I had him in the third round. And so that helium that he had, in my opinion, probably factored in a little bit as well," Watkins said about Betts' stock within the Red Sox organization, using a draft term—helium—which means his value was rising.

What also helped was that Watkins had established himself as a very good scout. The 2011 Draft would be his seventh with the organization and he had proven his evaluations were worth paying attention to.

"I think it speaks to the trust and trust is developed in an area scout over time," Watkins said. "And by that point in my Red Sox career, I guess I had developed a certain level of trust to where my initial report would generate some interest on the other side. The reader of the report would be able to look at the things I was saying, and then think to themselves, 'Yeah, okay, let's make sure we get some more eyes on this player.' And we started to get some guys come in, some cross checkers and special assistant guys, and to a man, they pretty much agreed with my feelings. And that helped me feel even more conviction that I was on the right path."

———

One of those people "on the other side" who read Watkins' reports was Tom Allison. He was brand new to the organization, having started on November 1, 2010. But he was far from a scouting novice. He had spent the previous four years as the scouting director of the Arizona Diamondbacks, overseeing a department that brought in players like Paul Goldschmidt, A.J. Pollock, and Wade Miley, among a host of other big leaguers. As is often the case in the industry, new management came in and wanted to bring in their own people, so Allison was dismissed from the D-backs, but was able to land on his feet as a Midwest regional crosschecker with the Red Sox. It was a continuation of a scouting career that began back in 1995, right after his playing days in the minor leagues ended, a long résumé he's still adding to.

Allison had spent seven seasons in a similar post with the Brewers, so he knew the drill. Like any scout coming in as a new guy in a supervisory position, he had to do two main things when he got started in the fall of 2010: Read through all the follow reports from the area scouts in his region and get to know the area scouts who wrote them.

"I remember reaching out, talking to Danny to ask, 'Hey, going into the year, who are your better feel guys that you're really excited about?'" said Allison, who joined the Los Angeles Dodgers as a special assignment scout in 2021. "And Mookie's name kept coming up."

So Alison really dove into the follow reports and the video the Red Sox had on Betts. His research taught him several things, including loving the fact that his initials were MLB. A player with any kind of major league bloodlines is always going to draw some attention, and Allison learned Betts' uncle is Terry Shumpert, who spent parts of 14 seasons in the big leagues. Allison put another check by his name when he read about how much Betts liked to talk hitting.

"This guy loves to talk about approach and what he was trying to do at the plate, despite what his other physical characteristics were," Allison recalled.

One of a veteran scout's biggest assets might be the relationships they form over the years in the game, ones that can become valuable resources. Case in point: Years ago, Allison had played against Tim Dulin. Dulin now runs one of the most elite travel teams in the country, the Dulin Dodgers. And, you guessed it, Mookie Betts played for the Dulin Dodgers in the summer of 2010 and again in 2011. That turned out to be just another positive recommendation for Allison to chew on.

Tim Dulin had started his elite travel ball program about 10 years earlier and the Dulin Dodgers already had a reputation for being one of the better programs in the country. Here is another example of previous relationships in baseball leading to something beneficial. One of Doolin's roommates when he played at the University of Memphis was Mike Morrison, who, as luck would have it, was the Overton high school baseball coach where Mookie Betts played.

"He had called me about Mookie and said, 'Hey, I got this special kid, and you need to meet him,'" Dulin recalled. "He and his dad were in Memphis during the winter playing in a high school basketball tournament... and I met with them. I was very impressed with [him] and his dad. And then then that summer, he played with me.

"You see guys come through, and I've been fortunate enough to have some really good players come through and his ability at that age to slow the game down and play with energy [stood out]. He wasn't very big back then. Heck, he's not big now. I had some infielders that were really, really good. And he was, at the time, a shortstop, and we were short in the outfield. And I said, 'Hey, can you play center field?' He was like, 'Yeah,' and he had never played it before. But he went out there and just did his thing. I knew at that point in time that as many players as you see, and you play as long as I did, he had that 'it' factor."

A few years later, Dulin was at the SEC tournament and talking to Red Sox general manager Ben Cherington, who was part of the front office as an assistant GM when Betts was drafted. As Dulin tells it, Cherington asked him whether Betts ever played the outfield for him. Dulin's response, of course, was, "Why, in fact he has," and proceeded to tell him the above story. Fast forward a couple of weeks and the Red Sox promoted Betts from Double-A Portland to Triple-A Pawtucket. And not long after that promotion, Betts started playing center field because that was more likely where there would be an opening in Boston, given the presence of Dustin Pedroia. Coincidence? Clearly, Dulin doesn't think so.

At this point, Allison already had put Betts on his must-see list. But there was one more piece of information that made him even more excited for spring trips to Tennessee. More often than not, initial follow lists are generated by one area scout only. That might be different if it's an elite-level prospect who plays at a variety of high-end showcase events over the summer. Betts wasn't quite at that level, but remember he did go to the East Coast Pro Showcase, where not only was he seen by all 30 teams, he was also seen by more than one Red Sox scout.

Tim Hyers was the Red Sox area scout in Georgia back then, before he went on to become the big league hitting coach. He was also at ECPS, so when Allison was creating a Mookie Betts file, he had strong evaluations not only from Watkins, but from Hyers as well. And that meant a lot to Allison.

"It speaks volumes as you're trying to understand new scouts, how they look at players, what they talk about, and when you kind of hear it in their voice, the inflection," Allison said. "They just wanted to continue to talk about some of the things that certain player, i.e., Mookie, did over the course of spending so much time with them. I personally put a heavy value on that. And so I was pretty excited to get to see him firsthand."

———

Over the course of the spring, while Watkins saw Betts five times, Allison managed to see him in three games, which is a large amount for a crosschecker who had a vast quantity of the eastern part of the United States to cross-check. Betts' location didn't hurt for any scouts who wanted to see him.

Just down the road from where Betts played was Vanderbilt University. As one of the best baseball programs in the country annually, it was always a must stop for scouts across all 30 teams. This year in particular, the Commodores had a very stacked roster, starting with first round pick Sonny Gray. Ironically, Gray would go one pick in front of the Red Sox's first selection of the 2011 draft, to the Oakland A's. It was a pretty deep class for college pitching that year and there was no doubt Gray was at least in the conversation for the Red Sox in the first round. After Gray was selected, the Red Sox took another college pitcher, Matt Barnes, who has been a valuable member of the big league bullpen in Boston for a number of years.

Vanderbilt had 12 players total drafted in 2011, so regional crosscheckers like Allison made frequent stops to watch them play. For Allison, it provided him the opportunity to spend more time with Betts than would be typical for someone in his position.

"You're going to spend a lot of time with Vanderbilt, but there's only a certain amount of time you need to watch them take batting practice, go through all the pre-game, that we would just run over and check in on Mookie," Allison said. "And so it was early in that year, Mookie's baseball season hadn't started, they had finished up basketball and he was going to hit in the cage. And that was the first time just to be around him. And again, I'm the only scout there and just sit and talk baseball [with him]."

As the spring wore on, Betts did nothing to turn the Red Sox away from their interest in him. Quite the contrary, it was his consistency game after game, at-bat after at-bat, that strengthened their conviction, even if he lacked the present strength to impact the ball in the way major league fans have grown accustomed to seeing. Who knows, maybe that lack of physicality helped the Red Sox, with other teams coming in for a look perhaps not being overwhelmed when they saw his size.

"Clearly Mookie was not a very strong physical player, you could project that coming in the years to come," Watkins said. "The thing that Mookie did was he rarely chased anything out of the zone. He always looked comfortable and balanced in the box. Very rarely did he swing and miss. And more than anything else, his swing was geared towards a through-the-middle approach, more often than not resulting in line drives.

"The quality of contact was definitely there and his ability to use the middle of the field. So many guys that we see now are only capable of hitting to the pull side. Watching him, his balance, his discipline, all those things, combined with the fact that he was able to make solid contact in the middle of the field, led me to believe that one day this guy would be a very good hitter."

There have been plenty of stories, especially about late-round picks, where an area scout stands alone in this kind of belief in a player. Watkins quickly knew others had his back. Having some unanimity in opinions on a player who was not on everyone's radar would certainly help when the decision was made to draft Betts.

"I vividly remember three scouts that, outside of Danny, were Mookie's champions, and so that spring, we had four scouts see Mookie, and they all loved him," said Amiel Sawdaye, then the Red Sox scouting director and now the D-backs senior vice president and assistant general manager. "Tommy Allison, [special assistant] Mark Wasinger, and Mike Rikard [then a national cross-checker and now the Red Sox vice president of scouting] were the four scouts that kind of all championed him at varying times."

"The one cross-check look that I was there for was with Mark Wasinger," Watkins recounts. "It was a playoff game and Mookie performed well, but he didn't have a great night. But Mark came away thinking, 'You know, Danny, you might be light on this guy.' Mark had been my cross-checker and then he was up to special assignment duty, so we had had some history. And when he gave me the indication that I might be light on Mookie, that really helped me out a lot."

————

While there wasn't industry wide interest in Betts, the Red Sox were not completely alone in showing interest. The Kansas City Royals had brought Betts in for a workout, but the one team Allison worried about the most was the San Diego Padres, mostly because anytime he showed up to check in on Betts, Padres crosschecker Sean Campbell was also there. When the draft came, and the rounds started to go by, that was the organization Allison was concerned would take the Tennessee high schooler before they could.

He wasn't wrong.

Campbell had just joined the Padres organization as the East Coast crosschecker the previous fall after having been an area scout in California for the Pittsburgh Pirates. Moving from the West Coast, Campbell had to decide where his home base would be, even if he spent much of the spring on the road. As luck would have it, he settled down in Nashville, a mere 10 to 15 minutes away from Overton High School.

Also living in Nashville was then area scout Mark Conner, who would go on to become San Diego's scouting director and currently holds a special assistant to the general manager job. One of the big benefits of living in Nashville for them both is that if they found out that Betts was, say, hitting in the cages, they could just run over and watch. Campbell (who ran an athlete development company called Loden Sports and was hired in 2022 by Major League Baseball to run the Draft League) recalled seeing Betts in three games but taking advantage of proximity to get a handful of extra glimpses. And he came in based on the recommendation of his area scout, Conner.

"It was not that I'm going to come into your area, and these are the guys I'm going to see," Campbell said. "It was more of, 'Hey, I'm coming into your area, who do you want me to see?'

"I think coming in not having any bias or history on seeing Mookie previously probably benefited me. I didn't have the 'Oh, he's only 5'8" or 5'9"' or I didn't have the 'Oh, it looks like he's maybe 135 pounds.' I didn't have any of those biases coming into it. What I was basing it off of was conversations with Mark and names that constantly came up."

Campbell and Conner both saw the control of the strike zone and the feel to hit that Watkins and Co. also had grown to like about Betts. And the more they saw of him, the more their opinion of him changed.

"I think the interest from there just kind of nudged and went up," Campbell said. "Maybe we started in the fifth or sixth round in a certain role with certain tools and then the next time you see him, it's a little bit better, you get a little bit more comfortable. Alright, let's bump this up. Let's bump that up. I think at the end of it, we both had him in the second round and going back and in retrospect, obviously, that was extremely light, you know?"

It begs one question, of course. If the Padres area scout and regional crosschecker had him in as a second rounder, if a national crosschecker saw him, if the scouting director came in to see a private workout, all of which occurred according to Campbell, how on earth did Mookie Betts not become a San Diego Padre?

It's a conversation Campbell and Conner have had over and over. In 2014, Conner was the scouting director and Campbell was the national crosschecker, giving them a slightly different vantage point of the dynamics in the draft room. They came to realize that in 2011, given the positions they had, they did everything they could to sway opinion in Betts' favor. Campbell recalled being very vocal in the room, but it was his first draft as a crosschecker and with this organization. He didn't want to place blame anywhere, especially because a dozen of the Padres' draft picks that year eventually went on to reach the big leagues. But it's clear he saw this as one of the biggest "one who got away" stories of his career.

"I don't know that we could have done anything more," Campbell said. "It sucks that this situation played out how it did. There was just this constant conversation about where you have to take him that I think permeates all draft rooms. I was pretty steadfast that to get him, you had to take him at the latest in the fifth round."

Perhaps if Campbell had pounded the table for the fourth round, we would have seen Betts in Petco Park instead of Fenway to begin his major league career. Because the Red Sox had the pick literally one in front of the Padres in the fifth round, we will never know if San Diego would have pulled the trigger had the Red Sox gone in a different direction. And in case you were curious, in the fourth round, the Padres took a right-handed pitcher from the junior college ranks, Cody Hebner, who spent most of his five seasons of time in the organization in A ball, never making it to the big leagues.

"I'd say probably 25% of my conversations with Mark Conner since I've been out of scouting has been about revisiting this," Campbell said.

———

When talking about hitters, there are the five tangible tools: hit, power, speed, arm, defense. There have been countless prospects drafted with the potential to have all five tools that can be found littered across the bin of forgotten minor league players. This is a hard game and just because someone has raw skills, it's far from a guarantee that it will translate to big league stardom. Remember Donavan Tate's big league career? No one does, because the super-talented No. 3 pick of the 2009 Draft never made it out of A ball in six minor league seasons.

How about Bubba Starling, the five-tooled phenom taken No. 5 overall in the same draft, 2001, when Betts went No. 172 overall? He did make it up to Kansas City, though he collected a grand total of 245 at-bats and posted a .544 OPS.

These examples are being brought up not to slight these players in any way. A sliver of the amateur baseball player world ever makes it to the pro ranks and the percentage who make it to the highest level is infinitesimal. Players like Tate and Starling are merely cautionary tale examples of how hard it is to predict future success, especially when looking at high school athletes making the leap to pro ball.

Teams have worked on all sorts of ways to measure a player's intangibles. They'll get to know the players, the families, work to learn about a player's drive, makeup, character. These are obviously extremely hard to quantify and a certain leap of faith is needed.

In addition to examining any potential off-the-field obstacles, trying to get a sense if a player's tools will translate as the game speeds up is equally challenging. With college players in big programs, there's more data that might correlate to future success. The gap for top high school players to traverse, especially from hotbed baseball states like Florida, California or Texas, has closed a bit, especially with scouts getting to see them against the top competition in the country in showcase events, typically the summer before their senior years.

By no means does this extra information create a guarantee. So the Red Sox worked on some proprietary testing to see if they could crack that mystery even a little. Working with an outside company, NeuroScouting, they had started to use computer programs and simulations to test things like decision-making, reaction time, and pitch recognition. They had employed some of this testing among minor leaguers to help measure these things, while giving prospects extra mental reps of a sort

It was still in its infancy and 2011 was the first time it was used on draftees. The thought was it might shed some light on how those tools might translate, even if a player—Mookie Betts, for example—didn't always face 90-plus mph fastballs in high school competition.

Watkins was the test administrator for Betts and kind of like a professor who proctors an exam for a colleague's class, he didn't know the subject matter nor how to score the test, so the fact that Betts' scores were off-the-charts wasn't apparent to him at the time.

"I didn't understand the neuroscouting, I just knew that I was supposed to give it," Watkins chuckled. "I knew how to administer it, but I've stood over the shoulder of many players who I thought did horribly on it and it turned out I was wrong. And I stood behind players and watched them take it and thought, 'Well, this guy's dominating this, this little game.' And turns out, they didn't do quite as well. So they never shared the results with me. I didn't know he scored as highly as he did until years later."

Betts didn't get it, either.

"I missed my lunch period because I was doing neuroscouting," Betts told the *Boston Globe* in 2015. "[Watkins] just said, 'Do this, don't think about the results.' I did what I could. It was just like, a ball popped up, tap space bar as fast as you could. If the seams were one way, you tapped it. If it was the other way, you weren't supposed to tap it. I was getting some of them wrong. I wasn't getting frustrated, but I was like, 'Dang, this is hard.'"

While the actual scores are unknown, and it feels like former and current Red Sox employees would take a cyanide pill before revealing those results, it is public knowledge that Betts did very, very well on the tests. Now, with this kind of testing much more prevalent around baseball, the testing fine-tuned over time and years of results archived, how Betts fared can be put into greater context. Back then? The Red Sox had faith it meant something. They just weren't sure what and depending on who you talk to, it had varying degrees of import.

"For me, it was kind of a cherry on top," said Rikard, who was then the national crosschecker and one of the four scouting members of the Mookie fan club. "We have the scouts that are saying this guy handles the bat really well, he doesn't swing and miss. He's got real, strong cognitive traits that show up in the batter's box as far as recognizing pitches and knowing what he's doing in the box. And then when you get these scores, they kind of are designed to encapsulate a lot of that, and then you see the scores are really good, too, it kind of confirms, to an extent, what we're seeing with our eyes. So for me, it was always kind of a cherry on top a little bit."

Sawdaye, the scouting director, also minimized the impact, though by no means did he diminish the efficacy of doing the testing.

"I think it's been somewhat sensationalized or exaggerated to some degree," he maintained. "Mookie Betts had a really high neuroscouting score. But it was a small piece of the puzzle.

"I believe in what the neuroscouting does, but at that point, we didn't know enough about neuroscouting to really carry enough weight to say, 'Oh, my God, this guy was one of the top scores that we've had...' But I think that that was a portion of the data that made us feel good."

Cherington, the assistant GM at the time, felt it was more essential, even if the lack of historical data collection made it tougher to analyze results:

> We certainly placed emphasis and thought it was really important to understand how hitters made decisions and felt really strongly that good, major league hitters just make good decisions. Yes, they're physically talented. Yes, they had a good swing as they had bat speed and strength. But they make good decisions. And we want to train that and develop that. We also want to try to identify that in amateur players.
>
> If you think about the trends in the draft, it's why a player who performs really well in the SEC gravitates up draft boards, because you have evidence of good decision making against good pitching.
>
> Of course, the further away you get from the major leagues, the harder that is to evaluate through performance, certainly for a high school player. And so the question was: Is there some way to assess a player's

ability to make decisions, good decisions, even if they haven't fully developed that skill, that they have the equipment, so to speak, to make good decisions, good swing decisions.

The truth is that when we started looking at that, and collecting information, we didn't really know yet if it was predictive. We knew that it was going to take a while to get gathered data and then see what would happen with those players to see if there was any correlation or predictive value to it. It wasn't a formal weight we put on it, but it was a piece of conversation. I can tell you that if we were lining up two high school players and everything else was pretty similar and one had really strong cognitive processing ability and one didn't, it ended up being a tiebreaker.

————

So, they had reports and recommendations from four trusted scouts, all of which was backed up by the data of this relatively new-fangled neuroscouting. How on earth, then, did the Red Sox wait until Round 5 to take Betts, nearly missing out on a player who would be a four-time All-Star, four-time Gold Glove winner, three-time Silver Slugger Award winner, an American League MVP and a World Series champion while wearing a Boston uniform?

The draft room is different for all 30 teams and often can take on a life of its own. At the very core, though, there generally will be the scouting director who runs the draft, the crosscheckers who can provide a national or regional perspective and, depending on the organization, some combination of area scouts who will advocate for players they want, especially if they've built some seniority and trust, and even more so as the rounds go by.

And don't forget the general manager and senior advisor types overseeing all of it.

This was a big draft for the Red Sox, with the chance to make a huge impact on their farm system. While they had lost their initial first-round pick to the Rays because they had signed Carl Crawford to a free-agent deal, they picked up two first rounders and two supplemental first-round selections as compensation for losing Victor Martinez and Adrian Beltre via free agency to the Tigers and Rangers, respectively. So Boston had four of the top 40 picks.

Additionally, this was the last year of the old draft system, often referred to as the "Wild West." Teams knew a new system was going to be put in place the following year and even if they didn't know the details yet, they were aware this would be the last draft where they could spend as freely as they saw fit. Since 2012, a bonus pool system has been in place that would have kept what the Red Sox, and other teams, did in previous years from happening. And spending in 2011 was off the charts as if MLB was having a going out of business sale.

The Red Sox, in a big market and always with a willingness to spend to win, knew all those extra picks could have a huge impact on the future of the organization. They could draft aggressively knowing ownership would likely write as many checks as they saw fit.

Boston took a balanced approach with those first four picks, taking a college pitcher with its first selection (Matt Barnes) and a college outfielder with its fourth (Jackie Bradley Jr.), with a pair of high schoolers in between who received bonuses above the MLB-recommended amounts for where they were picked (catcher Blake Swihart and lefty Henry Owens). And while this quartet had varying degrees of success, all four reached the big leagues.

As the draft turned to the second round, those on "Team Mookie" weren't quite anxious or ready to scream from the rooftops, but it's safe to assume they shifted in their chairs a bit more. The Red Sox would be picking just once per round, like every other team, from here on out, near the bottom of each round, and there would only be so many opportunities to get their guy and sign him away from his commitment to Tennessee.

They took a pair of other high school players, outfielder Williams Jerez and catcher Jordan Weems, in Rounds 2 and 3. Both also made it to the major leagues, though Weems did so as a relief pitcher. The fourth round began and the scouts who really wanted Betts to be a part of the organization started to get antsy. The Royals, the other team known to have real interest, picked closer to the top of the round, and took Florida high school right-hander Kyle Smith. One bullet dodged.

Everyone in the room knew the other team on Betts, the Padres, had the pick right *after* the Red Sox. So any more opportunities missed could hand him off to San Diego, or to Kansas City in the following round.

"There's a lot of different factors that go into this," Watkins said. "One of the things that we're always asked is, 'What teams are we competing with to get this guy?' And what's the player's attitude, what's more important to him, round or money? So you're going to reach a certain round, where if you take a player after that, he's going to feel like he's not valued. And so we got to the third round, and I felt like we might get a chance at the fourth if nobody else takes him."

They had the chance, and they passed, instead taking college right-hander Noe Ramirez, who, it should be pointed out, has carved out a nice career as a big league reliever. That definitely led to some raised eyebrows and furrowed brows.

"As we kept passing on Mookie, [Amiel Sawdaye] was looking at me, but my face said, 'You're the Director,'" said Allison, who in his first year with the club had to pick his spots. "'These are your calls, but we're going to take a college reliever right here?' No, I didn't actually say that.

"We took Noe Ramirez right before and Amiel looked over and said, 'We're going to get it, we're going to get it.' And I'm just sitting there. That's what you do as a supervisor, a crosschecker. You're waiting for your decision-makers to pull the tag."

There were a couple of variables that figured into how that fourth round went down. The Red Sox knew it would take extra money to sign Betts and like most people who are making an investment, ideally, you'd be able to check out first-hand where those dollars were going. And Sawdaye had never even laid eyes on Mookie Betts at that point. He had tried, but rain had spoiled his plan, so he was being asked to take a risk blindly and there's no way that didn't factor into Sawdaye's decision-making process.

"I think people would be lying if they said they it doesn't," Sawdaye said. "You always feel more comfortable with somebody you do or don't take that you've seen. That's no disrespect to the people that you work for or work with you. I just think it's human nature, you'd like to at least see what the kid looks like and get a chance to meet the kid."

Watkins, Allison, and company also weren't the only scouts in the room advocating for players. While they were trying to will a Mookie Betts selection into existence, there were other evaluators talking up Ramirez, who was coming off an outstanding year in Cal State Fullerton's rotation.

"We're kind of lined up to take [Betts] and one of our scouts comes in and says, 'Hey, we could take Noe Ramirez here. He slid and we really like Noe; he is a college performer and he'll sign here. He's a pretty low risk major league player,'" Sawdaye recalled. "At that point, I had to make that decision because I was getting pulled in two different directions. I had one guy telling me take Noe Ramirez and you know he's a big leaguer. And then

I had other guys telling me we're going to lose Mookie Betts if we wait. And I just kind of played the odds.

"I remember saying, 'I will take Noe here,' and thankfully Mookie was there in the fifth, and Noe's carved out a really good career. Because I remember the look that I got from the scouts in the room who really wanted Mookie. I think they would have probably wrung my neck if we lost him, and I don't know if I would be able to live with myself as a scouting director who lost out on Mookie Betts. We took a kind of a calculated risk and it worked out."

They wouldn't know that for another tension-filled 30 picks. The Padres could have taken Betts with the next pick but opted for junior college right-hander Cody Hebner. No one was celebrating, but a quick exhale may have been permitted.

"We got through the fourth round, and I'm thinking, 'Okay, we need to do this now because Mookie, number one, needs to feel valued,'" Watkins said. "And number two, there's only going to be so much bonus money to hand out. And we need to go ahead and get him now."

There was one more hurdle to clear: the Royals' fifth-round pick. Watkins had a sense that both Kansas City and San Diego, while willing to spend, didn't have the same deep pockets as Boston did, and the fear one of those teams would draft Betts, then not be able to sign him, was very real.

The Royals did go with a high school infielder in that round, a Texas shortstop named Patrick Leonard and they somewhat ironically went over slot to sign him for $600,000. Leonard never made it to the big leagues and might be best known for being traded to the Rays in 2012 as part of the James Shields deal.

Finally, 16 picks later, Sawdaye finally pulled Betts' tag and the pick was announced and the angst cleared the draft room in a hurry. Hindsight can be 20–20, but Sawdaye can't help but shake his head at just how fortunate he was.

"It was very intense," he said. "And I tell people probably one of the biggest mistakes I made was not taking Mookie Betts higher in the draft because I almost lost him. I used to go back and re-read the reports and if you really sift through the reports, we probably should have taken him in the first or second round, given the way we wrote about him."

––––––––

Drafting a player is one thing; signing him can be quite another. Especially in those days when there was no penalty for not signing a pick. (In today's system, you lose the bonus slot amount from your overall pool to spend if you don't sign a player in the top ten rounds.) And most players, if they had any leverage at all, like, say, a commitment to a school in the SEC, would wait until the last minute to sign right at the August 15 deadline.

Before the bonus pool system was implemented, it was always a good idea to have a sense of a player's signability. You always wanted to avoid taking a player, especially early, who didn't want to sign or would break the bank to do so. But without the limitations on draft spending like baseball has now, that bank was a bit malleable, especially for a team with resources like the Red Sox. (It wasn't limited to the big market clubs; some teams prioritized spending on the draft to build a farm system precisely because they didn't have the means to sign big leaguers to huge multi-year contracts. In 2011, the Pirates not only signed No. 1 overall pick Gerrit Cole for $8 million, but they also surprised the baseball world by inking Josh Bell for $5 million in the second round.)

The Red Sox, with all those extra picks, had a lot of balls in the air to juggle and nearly all of them didn't land until the 11th hour of that deadline, which was at midnight on August 15. Boston had taken six high schoolers, who generally have more leverage because of the possibility of heading to college, in the first seven rounds. Trying to figure out if they could afford all of them started with the area scout, who would try to ascertain what a player's bonus figure might be. It wasn't uncommon for it to escalate up the ladder, which is exactly what happened in this case.

"That was something that was handled above my level," Watkins said. "I was responsible to give them an idea of what I thought he would sign for. I missed. I thought he would sign at a lower level than what he ended up signing for. But by that point, his advisors had really kind of taken the ball on that and they were dealing with the front office."

The front office, at least, was able to use the time to get to know Betts a bit better. Remember, Sawdaye had never actually gotten the chance to see him play, so this was a chance for him to get a sense of who exactly he might be advocating to sign a large check to. He had two main opportunities to spend time with Betts.

The first came at Fenway Park. The Red Sox had started a tradition where they would invite all their draftees to play a game in their storied ballpark, regardless of round or if they were going to sign. For example, the Red Sox took Hunter Renfroe out of high school in Round 31 of the 2010 Draft and he attended the game, known as the Family Classic, that summer. He didn't sign and instead headed to Mississippi State, where he would emerge as a first-round pick three years later.

"So Mookie came up, I want to say that was probably the beginning of July," Sawdaye said. "He came up decked out in Tennessee gear and he played in that game. So that was really the first time a lot of us got to lay eyes on him."

Whether Betts' clothing choice was a bargaining ploy can be debated. But there is no question that his decision to return to the Dulin Dodgers to play some more was made in the hopes it would help him come deadline time.

"I think we kind of had a game plan," Dulin said. "At the time, the draft was the early part of June and because he had not played a lot on the circuit and a lot at a high level, we used it as the ability for him to make some money from the draft until that signing, until he had to decide. And he actually did because I won't go into what the initial offer was, but it was substantially lower than what he ended up getting. And I think part of that was that the Red Sox were able to spend a lot of time to determine, 'Is he worth what he's asking for or not?'"

It turned out to be mutually beneficial, even if the Red Sox had to eventually reach into the pocketbook a bit deeper to come up with the $750,000 they gave Betts to sign. That's because it provided an open line of communication, one that a veteran scout like Tom Allison was sure to use, staying in contact with his old friend Tim Dulin to make it clear the Red Sox did plan to sign their fifth rounder.

That became more important because as the summer wore on, the University of Tennessee put on the hard sell. It was an entirely new coaching staff in Knoxville, one that didn't recruit Betts. Allison made sure to reach out to another member of the baseball fraternity, Bill Masiello, who new head coach Dave Serrano had hired to be the Volunteers' head coordinator and hitting coach. Allison wanted them to know of their intention to bring Betts into the Red Sox organization, but he also knew Masiello would like what he saw once he witnessed Betts play.

"He had never seen Mookie Betts," Allison said. "But he's playing for the Dulin Dodgers.... He goes down and Bill's a very good evaluator. I know at that time he was super, super intrigued, like, 'We need to keep this guy.' And that's where some of the obstacles started to float. It was the comparisons of some of the other players that we had selected in past drafts, and how much money we had given them. So that's when different information started flowing towards Mookie, from the new regime there at the University of Tennessee."

So far this doesn't sound so mutually beneficial, does it? But while this was going on, Sawdaye also used the time to not only see Betts play for the Dulin Dodgers himself in Georgia, but spend the day with Betts, bring him to a Greenville (at the time the Low-A affiliate for the Red Sox) game against the Rome Braves, get to see what made Mookie Betts tick.

"It really made me feel a lot more comfortable with who he was," Sawdaye said. "He's a lot of who he is today, very humble, very confident.

"I tried to be very respectful of the situation because you're not going to negotiate with a player without his representation. We just talked a little bit about the minor leagues and college and he just said, 'Look, I have two really good opportunities. And if I go to University of Tennessee, I'm fine with that. I think I'll be really good and I'll be in this position in a couple years. And if I sign, I feel the same way. And so, I hope it works out.' I think he wanted to sign and I think he was alluding to, 'I hope I get the money I want, but if I don't, I'm fine with that.' I thought it was a really mature way of attacking the situation."

That didn't mean it was all smooth sailing with an easy negotiation. Things stalled at around $500,000, with Betts asking for a quarter-million more and the Red Sox weren't sure what to do. But as the deadline approached, general manager Theo Epstein provided a breakthrough moment when he asked Sawdaye and his staff what kind of player they thought Betts could be. When the answer was that they believed he could be a good everyday player, maybe one who could make an All-Star team for a competitive team, Epstein simply said: If you think that, sign the guy.

It made even more sense because they could spread the bonus around. There was a rule back then that made it easier, financially, for a team to sign a multi-sport athlete. Now, Betts wasn't getting recruited to play basketball for big programs, but he had drawn interest. That meant the Red Sox could pay his bonus over five years, instead of all at once. In the end, they paid the bonus at $150,000 per year over those five years. In other words, it turned out to be an extra $50K a year more than they were stuck on to bring in one of the most exciting talents in MLB.

What Sawdaye didn't know until years later was that he and the Red Sox had lost a game of chicken with Betts and his reps. It was 2015, when Betts was getting that final bonus installment ad was establishing himself as a bona fide star. The team was in Kansas City and Sawdaye was with the team. Sawdaye, Betts and then-bench coach Torey Lovullo were standing in the clubhouse kitchen, taking about the draft negotiations. Sawdaye remembers the exchange like it was yesterday:

> Lovullo: Take me back when you got drafted. What was your final number you would have signed for at the end of the day?
> Betts: 500. I just got my last payment, but I probably would have signed for 500. But I got an extra 250.

"At the time, Mookie was just starting to go off," Sawdaye recalled. "I said, 'Believe me, I'm sure the Red Sox are just fine paying you an extra 250 right now.'"

Chapter 5

Charlie Blackmon

"**I told him** I was a two-way player, which wasn't true."

This was the lie... well perhaps lie is too harsh... this was the truth-bender that launched Charlie Blackmon's professional career.

You see, when Blackmon arrived at the fledgling Texas Collegiate League in the summer of 2007, it was to do what those in baseball who knew him at that point had thought was his ticket: pitch. If it weren't for his résumé-expansion, a former big league outfielder who coached him that summer and an elbow issue that got this baseball rat to do anything just to play more, it's possible we may not have ever seen Blackmon, the All-Star, the Silver Slugger Award winner, and the National League batting champion.

"I think it was more that I failed as a pitcher and the hitting thing was a plan B," Blackmon explained. "But there was a time I felt like I was going to be a pitcher. That is what I was working towards. It wasn't until that door closed that I really tried to pursue hitting."

Like with most high school players, Blackmon did both pitch and hit at North Gwinnett High in Georgia. But scouts who covered that area back in 2004 typically only remember the tall, athletic and projectable left-handed pitcher. There weren't as many showcase events back then as there are these days and Blackmon, who divided some of his time playing football and basketball, didn't get to much of what was available. For example, there is record of just one Perfect Game event he ever attended: the 2004 World Wood Bat Association 18U National Championship played at the East Cobb Complex in Marietta, about 40 minutes away from Blackmon's hometown in Georgia.

And to give you an idea of just how overlooked Blackmon was as a prospect to get invited to the big events, that tournament took place AFTER the 2004 Draft, when he had already graduated high school. This wasn't a kid scouts were flocking to see, like, say, Justin Verlander, who was a college right-handed pitcher at the time who ended up being the No. 2 overall pick in that '04 Draft. There were dozens of scouts at each of Verlander's starts, radar guns in hand, charting each pitch.

Though Blackmon didn't have any Division I college offers coming out of high school—his one and only offer to play beyond high school came from Young Harris College, a two-year school also in Georgia, he wasn't completely ignored by pro scouts. The Florida Marlins took a late-round flyer in the 28th round on Blackmon's upside on the mound, but the pro game wasn't something he would seriously consider for another few years.

"I didn't come on to the scene or become anybody of note until probably halfway through my senior year as a lefty on the mound, kind of tall," he said. "I wasn't that impressive, I was probably mid 80s but athletic and honestly I was surprised when I got drafted.

"I signed the first collegiate offer that I got from Young Harris College. That was the first and only offer I received. I was just happy that somebody gave me a chance."

The phone wasn't ringing with college offers, but he didn't go completely unnoticed. There was at least one area scout at the time who found his athleticism and left-handedness on the mound intriguing. Brian Bridges had begun a scouting career in 2001 that has since taken him all the way up to the Scouting Director's chair with the Braves. The 2004 Draft was his first with the Marlins and he was their area scout in Georgia during Blackmon's senior year.

"He's a 6'3" athlete whose body changed as he matured, but it's basically the same body it was as a youngster," said Bridges, who made his way from the Marlins to the Braves, the team he would eventually serve as scouting director for, and on to the Giants, serving as San Francisco's national crosschecker starting in 2019. "And he was easy 87–88 mph with good shape to it, plus he had the makings of a plus breaking ball, and he's left-handed. Well let's check all the boxes: one, we have an athlete; two, he's left-handed; three, he can spin a breaking ball."

That, in a nutshell, is every scout's dream. An athlete on the mound who is projectable—a player who will grow into his body and throw harder in the future—could be a future Clayton Kershaw or Madison Bumgarner. Or maybe David Price is a better example, a lefty who was interesting in high school and was taken in the 19th round of the 2004 Draft by the Dodgers, but went on to Vanderbilt and emerged three years later as the No. 1 overall pick. Blackmon didn't necessarily have that kind of ace-like potential, but it was clear he needed more development time and had considerable upside.

"He wasn't ready to go out then, but we still had the draft-and-follow, so we went ahead and fired in the 28th round. [Scouting director] Stan Meek took him for me, and he marched on to Young Harris College with Rick Robinson," Bridges recalled.

The draft-and-follow was a tool many teams used back then to keep an eye on intriguing talent like Blackmon. When a player was selected back then, teams had almost an entire year, up until the week before the following year's draft, to sign him. With a raw high schooler, a team might roll the dice with a late-round pick, like the Marlins did with Blackmon, then track his progress at a junior college the following spring. If a high schooler headed to a four-year school, he wouldn't be available for the draft for another three years. (Occasionally two years. Running the risk of getting too deep into the weeds here with draft rules minutia, a player can be drafted as a sophomore if they're 21 years old at the time of the draft.) A team would lose the rights to sign a player if he headed to a four-year school, but those rules didn't apply for junior colleges. There have been some All-Star caliber players to come from the draft-and-follow, like Andy Pettitte, taken in the 22nd round of the 1990 Draft by the Yankees out of the Texas high school ranks, then signing him the following May after he threw well at San Jacinto Junior College, or Mark Buehrle, a 38th-round pick of the White Sox in 1990 who went from his high school in Missouri to Jefferson College, a two-year school in the Show-Me State and joined Chicago the following spring. Those two southpaws won a combined 470 games over very lengthy careers.

———

Now it's not like Bridges or anyone else felt certain Blackmon would go on to be like either of those southpaws, but he and the Marlins saw enough to see what might transpire at Young Harris in 2006. Young Harris had recently produced first-rounder Nick Markakis, ironically a two-way player some liked on the mound who went on to play 15 years in the big leagues.

    Blackmon did some good things as a freshman at the Georgia junior college, winning seven games and striking out 49 in

44⅔ innings, though he also walked 24 and finished with a 5.24 ERA across 17 appearances, half of them starts. He was the tournament MVP as the Mountain Lions won the 2005 GJCAA State Championship. There was some interest from the Marlins in signing him, but they couldn't work that out.

"[That] fall, the velocity started to creep up a little bit," Bridges said. "He was touching 91 and we started to get excited about how Charlie's arm was working and the things he was doing. As the course of the next spring went on, he really didn't materialize. It was just that his arm wasn't bouncing back from start to start or inning to inning."

The Boston Red Sox saw enough to take a flier on him in the 20th round of the '05 Draft, and Blackmon got an invite to pitch in the elite college summer Cape Cod League, where he finished with a 3.42 ERA in 11 games, all but two in relief. He only gave up 18 hits in 26⅓ innings, striking out 24. But he also walked 22 and he headed back to Young Harris, pro ball still not on his mind.

But hitting started to be, though it was still very much a secondary skill. He won eight games and K'd 89 on the mound, finishing with a 3.39 ERA, but again carried an inflated walk rate (just over five walks per nine). But he also got at-bats as a designated hitter. Some of it came as a result of the arm trouble that would lead to the end of his career as a pitcher; much of the reason was an anemic Young Harris offense that was trying to find ways to score runs any way it could.

"Halfway through my sophomore year we were struggling hitting and our coach brought some of the more athletic pitchers out just to shock-and-awe scare the offense," Blackmon recalled. "And they let some of these pitchers hit BP to let our offense know they are replaceable. I had a pretty impressive BP so I got to DH a little bit my sophomore year. But I did not play a position. I was not really a hitter."

For a hitter who has gone on to build a career largely around one of the most advanced approaches at the plate in the big leagues, back then it was pretty simple: See the ball, hit the ball.

"I remember my coach telling me he wanted me to hit like a pitcher. 'Don't hit like a hitter. Just go up there and swing the bat. Don't think, you're a pitcher [and] we're going to put you in there to hit here and there.'"

It was just a glimpse, 98 at-bats according to Young Harris records, but he did hit .327/.385/.490. Bridges remembers talking to Rick Robinson at the time about how he was going to use Blackmon both ways, a kind of mini-Markakis. That didn't make anyone sit up and take notice at the time, though, and Blackmon wasn't drafted for a third time in 2006.

Of course, had Bridges been paying closer attention when scouting him back in high school, perhaps Blackmon would be winning a batting title, Silver Slugger Awards, and attending All-Star Games for the Marlins.

"He was playing in the outfield and the coach guaranteed me he would throw before the end of the game," Bridges recalled. "What was ironic about this whole story... we are watching him play the outfield. He's bouncing around and Mike Cadahia [now the Washington Nationals director of international operations, then the Marlins regional cross-checker] goes, 'I kind of like his swing.' I was like, 'Yeah he is smoking the ball over the yard.'"

"We always have these conversations. We just didn't see that or we didn't see that coming but all indications were there and we just kept overlooking it.... He always had a good swing and he was always athletic and he could always throw and he could run. I mean there's a lot of athleticism there with Charlie. It's just everybody saw the left-handed athletic arm and really pushed him to be that.

"When he was a senior in high school, Mike C nailed it. If you are going to give credit to anybody, my regional cross checker said, 'Hey man, we could really [draft-and-follow] him as an outfielder.' I guess we were both caught in between on it and we took him as a pitcher and that kind of started the avenue for Charlie just as far as the pitching went."

That pitching avenue wasn't closed just yet. While Blackmon didn't get drafted after his second year at Young Harris, he did get something that had been lacking previously: a Division I offer. And it came from ACC power Georgia Tech.

———

Danny Hall has been doing this a really long time. He's been a Division I head coach for more than three decades. And he's been at Georgia Tech's helm since the first term of the Bill Clinton presidency, joining the Yellow Jackets in 1994. He became the school's winningest coach all the way back in 2005 and is in the top 20 among all Division I coaches in career victories, a number that surpassed 1,300 in 2021. He's been to the College World Series, won several conference titles, and has seen more than a dozen first round picks come through his program.

It isn't really necessary to roll out his résumé, but his bona fides certainly add some weight to his opinions. And he liked Charlie Blackmon. Liked him a little bit in high school, liked him more after his first year at Young Harris, especially following his Cape Cod League performance, and was happy to add him to the program after Blackmon's sophomore season.

"At the time [high school], he pretty much felt like he wasn't ready to go play at our level and so he kind of indicated to us he was going to go to Young Harris," Hall said. "So we kind of followed him up there. He had a pretty good first year there… and I know we had some conversations with him about coming but he indicated he wanted to stay both years at Young Harris. So we just kind of continued the conversations and again all of the conversations were him being a left-handed pitcher in our program.

"So finally after his second year there, he said he was going to come. We had him on the radar pretty early but it was more him wanting to make sure he was ready to come and compete for a spot either in our rotation or just on our team to be a pitcher."

It would add to the legend of Danny Hall's career if he could claim he saw Blackmon's potential in the batter's box. But he knows better than to taunt the baseball gods with some revisionist history. Truth is, even with Blackmon's occasional DH duties at Young Harris, Hall didn't even know his new recruit could hit. If it weren't for elbow issues, he may never have found out.

Finding left-handed pitching at any level, let alone in one of the best Division I conferences in the country, is never easy and demand always outstrips supply. So, the Yellow Jackets were thrilled to welcome this big, athletic southpaw with two solid years of JUCO experience into the fold. It became apparent, relatively quickly, that he wasn't the guy they thought they were getting.

Blackmon had started to experience some elbow problems during his second year at Young Harris, some tendinitis he kept hoping would just go away. In his first attempts to show Hall and his staff what he could do, his velocity had dropped considerably.

"He had gone from the upper-80s/low-90s to now here's a guy who threw 84–85 mph with not a lot of command, not a really good breaking ball," Hall recalled. "We were kind of scratching our heads a little bit, like 'Where is this guy going to fit in as a pitcher for us?'"

Pitchers get hurt, a lot. But it's not like a car that doesn't run right after you drive it off the lot. It's not like Hall could return Blackmon to Young Harris and ask for a refund. So Blackmon worked to get back to the pitcher he was previously. And worked. And worked. And worked. The guy everyone sees in the big leagues playing like it's his last game on earth? That's who he's always been and he had the same approach to proving to Hall he belonged.

He rehabbed, he went to see Dr. James Andrews for a consult to make sure he didn't need surgery. He spent as much time as possible on a mound trying to regain his feel for his craft. All of that work led to exactly one appearance in 2007 where he allowed two runs on two hits and two walks in one inning. He didn't join the team on the road because travel rosters were limited and, frankly, he wasn't ready to produce.

Not that he didn't try, though most of his effort came solo and his best friend may have been a plastic dummy.

"The legend of it is, and he can speak to it more, is he would go up in our cages because we had an indoor mound up there and just throw balls into a net," Hall said. "He was constantly working, trying to get back to where he was and ultimately be able to contribute to our team."

"I was able to rehab and avoid surgery but I just felt like it took me too long to come back," Blackmon said. "My arm slot felt weird. I wasn't throwing nearly as hard. I wasn't throwing strikes. I had a really tough time at Georgia Tech as a red shirt. I wasn't traveling. I was home by myself half the time on campus in the cage throwing bullpens with a dummy plastic hitter standing in there. Like I was trying to figure it out as best I could and I couldn't turn the corner. It was just a really tough year for me and I was able to obtain a medical redshirt that first year."

After suffering through that miserable 2007 year, the plan was to find a place for Blackmon to make up for lost time. The Cape didn't make sense—too competitive for a guy basically on a rehab assignment. He needed reps more than anything so Hall sent him to the fledgling Texas Collegiate League for innings.

———

The Texas Collegiate League began just a few years prior to Blackmon's arrival, a group of eight teams in North Texas towns forming a wood-bat college league in 2004. It had already helped produce some draft talent, with 70 TCL alumni getting selected in the 2007 Draft, which took place right before Blackmon started playing there, the headliner being right-hander Jake Arrieta.

That summer, Blackmon played against and with future big leaguers like All-Star Brandon Belt and Bryan Price, who has made more of a name for himself as a pitching coach than a player. At the time, of course, the hope was that Blackmon could be more like Price, who pitched at Rice University and was the 45th overall selection of the 2008 Draft by the Red Sox, than Belt, a left-handed hitter who went from San Jacinto Junior College to the University of Texas to the San Francisco Giants, who took him in the fifth round of the 2009 Draft.

For his part, Blackmon wasn't even dreaming of pro ball at that point. He really only wanted to play the game again, in any way possible.

"I just wanted to get back on the field," Blackmon said. "I didn't have any aspirations of playing at the next level, I was just missing baseball having not played that year at Georgia Tech and wanting to get on the field. So I told Rusty Greer—who was our coach out there—I told him I was a two-way player, which wasn't true. I hadn't been hitting, you know, hadn't been playing any defense since high school really. So I just grasped at anything trying to get on the field in any way possible."

Yes, it's *that* Rusty Greer, the former Texas Ranger who played in the big leagues for nine years and retired with a .305 career batting average and 1166 career hits. The one who drove in 100 runs three different times and never hit below .270 in his career. In other words, the guy knows a thing or two about hitting, particularly from the left side.

He thought he was getting a left-handed pitcher and a DH. That's what he was told, anyway, and the desperate-to-compete Blackmon confirmed it. Though Blackmon hit in the middle of the Colleyville LoneStars lineup as a designated hitter when he wasn't pitching, the mound was still the focus point, first in long relief to build up innings and then in some starts.

"We put him on the mound; he was 88–90," said Greer, who now runs a baseball school that focuses on teaching young players defense. "Just a short breaking ball, it wasn't a real impressive hammer or sharp slider. He had a pretty good changeup. To me he was just what I would consider at the big league level an average left-hander, a late-inning guy maybe one or two hitters here and there. So not that he was doing badly, he was doing well."

"I was still really wanting to hold on to the pitching things because I thought that was my potential," Blackmon said. "I came in as a left-handed pitcher; it's a wood-bat league. I had never actually swung a wood bat really, so I was trying to get used to that thing."

Greer immediately liked Blackmon's swing, though he didn't realize at the time it was not something he'd been doing in recent years.

"I did not know that and the only reason that I thought he could swing the bat a little bit was when he was taking BP and I liked his stroke," Greer recounted. "Had I known he hadn't swung a bat in two years I would have probably been more impressed with his stroke. Because it was a good left-handed stroke with some juice and we're using wood bats. He is hitting the ball right on the button and of course we don't know the whole history of every player.

"And so he wanted to get some at-bats but his main goal was to come in and pitch. Because of what he did in his BP and the way he swung a bat he was pretty much a regular in our line up every day."

In the early stages of the summer, Blackmon was still a pitcher who evidently could swing the bat a little. The next shift in his career trajectory didn't come until Greer's eye caught the lefty getting his post-pitching running in. Remember that scene in *The Natural* when Pop Fisher, the manager of the last place New York Knights, watches Roy Hobbs take batting practice for the first time? He goes and takes a drink of water from the rusty water fountain and is so distracted by Hobbs' talent that he doesn't even realize it's the same water he spit out just recently. It might be overdramatic to say Greer had exactly the same response, but there's no question he stopped in his tracks when he saw Blackmon run. Greer tells it best, recalling the conversation he had with his assistant coach, Alan McDougal:

> We were working on the field after a game and Charlie had pitched. And he was the only one there. I was dragging circles around the infield and McDougal was raking up around the bases. And I made a circle and Charlie was running sprints. He was running about 60–65-yard sprints. So he took off and I am dragging the circle and I'm watching him run and I'm thinking man this kid can run a little bit. So I made another circle and he walked back and I made another circle and he took off again and I watched him and I said this kid is running. He's not running a little bit, he is moving. So the third time he goes back and I made another circle and I actually stopped and I watched him. He walks back again and I whistled over to McDougal the assistant coach and I pointed out and I said watch this. He took off running and he looked at me kind of wide eyed. I said I know man the kid can fly.

Greer called Blackmon over after he was done running and asked him if he ever thought about playing the outfield. According to Greer, Blackmon responded with a can-do answer that he's carried with him throughout his career.

"This is Charlie Blackmon probably still to this day. He said, 'I'll do whatever you want me to do. I just want to play.'"

The next step was to get him to take fly balls in center field during batting practice over the next few games as a crash course to get him ready to play in a game. He had moved from the middle of the lineup to the top because he was probably the fastest player on the LoneStars and after a few days of shagging fly balls, he's hitting leadoff and playing center. The Hollywood script would have the first ball hit to him and he makes a diving play, but it wasn't that far off.

"It was fairly early on the ball with him playing defense for us. There was a ball in the right-center-field gap—I can see it to this day—and he ran a long way for it and caught it," Greer said. "I turned to the assistant coach and said this kid ain't no pitcher, he's an outfielder. So one thing led to another and he wound up playing center field every day for us."

Athletes can be stubborn. And Blackmon, after all, had been drafted as a pitcher, twice. And recruited by Georgia Tech on the mound. And sent to Colleyville to work on that craft. It wasn't necessarily a slam dunk that he'd want to stop pitching and suddenly become an outfielder. But maybe this is where the baseball gods intervened in bringing Blackmon together with someone with the MLB résumé Greer had. What his summer league manager had to say carried a lot of weight because of what he had accomplished at the highest level.

"He told me that he thought I was going to be a much better hitter or outfielder than I would ever be as a pitcher," Blackmon recalled. "I am glad it was him because I am pretty hard-headed, I kind of like things my way and had it been somebody else without as much experience I could have maybe just blown them off. But Rusty was adamant about it. He really cared; he was really invested in that team. He spent a lot of time with me and really seemed to believe in me.

"I really had nothing to lose I wasn't really getting better at pitching at this point. I thought, 'Hey, this guy seems to know what he's doing. He's got a lot of experience; he was certainly a great player. Maybe he's right. Maybe I can believe in this a little bit.'"

Greer certainly believed in it, but don't ask him to take any curtain calls for his role in Blackmon's career.

"By no means do I take credit for Charlie Blackmon's career or anything he's done. That is all on Charlie. Charlie was a guy— and still is—one of the hardest workers, a 'I will do anything you want me to' guy to be able to play. Just like the night we were there watching him run. He was the last guy there running under the lights.

"I would like to think I played a little part in his path but Charlie has done really well for himself and made a huge name for himself. I think it all starts with his work ethic and the way he wanted to play. He didn't care where it was; I probably could have put him at first base or shortstop and he would have gone out and tried. But he's done really well for himself."

———

Greer did one more thing before passing the baton. He called Danny Hall back at Georgia Tech. The message was a simple one: I'm not going to tell you how to run your program, but that southpaw you sent here? You may want to hand him a bat instead.

"Coach Hall probably wouldn't remember this conversation but I said, 'I know he came as a pitcher but he's an outfielder. He's playing center for us and doing really well.' I just said, 'If

you want to get the most out of him I'd put him in the outfield.'
He said, 'Okay, I'll take that under advisement.'"

Coach Hall certainly did remember the conversation. He was
with one of his sons at a summer baseball tournament when his
phone rang and he recognized the Dallas area code, thanks to the
fact that former Yellow Jacket start Mark Teixeira was playing
for the Texas Rangers at the time.

"So I answer the call and it's Rusty Greer and he's like,
'Danny I don't know if you know who I am but I am Rusty
Greer.' And I said, "Well, if it's the Rusty Greer who played for
the Rangers, I know who you are.'"

Like Blackmon, Hall figured, "If Rusty Greer thinks this is
worth a shot, maybe it's worth a shot."

"I just kind of said, 'If you are telling me I need to take a
look at it we are going to take a look at it.' So that was the seed
planted in my mind by Rusty Greer that this guy may be able
to help us as an outfielder and a hitter," Hall said.

Fall baseball in college is often a time to tinker, to try a new
position, to experiment. It was a perfect environment to see if
Rusty Greer knew what he was talking about. When Blackmon
had first gotten to Georgia Tech after transferring, he did tell
the coaching staff he could hit a little, but after watching him
take some swings in batting practice that first fall, they told him
to stick to pitching.

But this time he was more prepared. And more confident
after his very successful summer and Greer's verbal letter of recommendation. Everyone around Blackmon, from the coaching
staff to his roommates, were skeptical. Luckily, Hall let Blackmon
ease into competition by letting him get his first at-bat against…
David Duncan.

Duncan had already been drafted twice, once out of high
school in 2005 and once as a draft-eligible sophomore who was
eligible at Georgia Tech in 2007. He'd be the Yellow Jackets'

ace the following spring and he was 6′9″. Oh, and he was also left-handed, sure to give any lefty hitter fits, let alone one who had just started hitting again 10 minutes ago, relatively speaking.

"We're getting ready to play our first intrasquad game, and me being the smart you-know-what that I am, I'm like, 'Okay, Charlie Blackmon, I'm going to make you face our number one pitcher…. Let's see how you do against Duncan,'" Hall said.

How did he do against Duncan? He took him deep. Like, way out of the ballpark.

"He fell behind me 2–0 and the first swing anybody saw me take, he threw a fastball down the middle and I hit it pretty far, I crushed it," Blackmon said. "I heard somebody say the big man upstairs was looking out for me that day. I was super nervous, hoping for the best. Picked the worst draw with our Friday night pitcher. I might've gotten a little bit lucky."

In intrasquad games, you don't round the bases on a home run like in the regular season. You're expected to just peel off after you round first and return to the dugout, like it's no big deal. Blackmon did his best to nonchalant the fact he had just taken Georgia Tech's ace deep on his first-ever swing as a Yellow Jacket, but he did manage to sneak a peek over to see what Hall's reaction was.

"He was completely beside himself laughing and I guess that gave me the opportunity to get a few more at-bats in fall practice."

"It was quick and obvious as the fall went on that not only was this guy going to play but he was going to start and that he could really hit," Hall said. "He just had a really good knack for putting the barrel on the ball and back then he was an elite runner."

Hall had seen enough talented players come out of his program to recognize even that fall that perhaps Blackmon had the chance to play beyond his final year at Georgia Tech. So much so that when new Rockies area scout Alan Matthews was setting up offseason meetings with potential draftees, Hall recommended he add Blackmon to a list that included Duncan and Chris Hicks, a right-hander with a big arm. Both Duncan and Hicks would get drafted by the Astros the following June, Duncan in the fifth round, Hicks in Round 14.

"When my first knowledge of Charlie and who he was and what he was capable of really began was that conversation I had with Danny Hall that afternoon before the '08 season," Matthews said.

It might seem counter-intuitive to think that ignorance could be an advantage for a scout. After all, area scouts are the first line of defense in amateur player acquisition, tasked with knowing any and every player in the region they are assigned to cover. The gut reaction would be to think that the fact Alan Matthews didn't know who Charlie Blackmon was would be a detriment. Veteran scouts obviously knew him from his high school days and had track record; some even had relationships with him.

In this case, though, knowledge was not power.

"The fancy term for it now is 'anchor positions' on certain players," said Matthews, who is now a regional cross-checker for the Los Angeles Dodgers. "We have history with them or we have some preconceived ideas about what they are and who they are and sometimes we tend to scout with one eye closed. I know I have been guilty of it since."

In this case, though, not knowing was a gift. As a rookie scout, Matthews didn't even know Blackmon had been a heralded pitcher earlier in his career who was suddenly making a shift to salvage his college career. He only knew him as Charlie Blackmon, fourth-year junior outfielder at Georgia Tech, though he was one who made Matthews take note of him before he saw him take a single at-bat.

"He definitely made an impression in terms of his character and the way he conducted himself," Matthews said about that fall interview. "His professionalism, his humility, he was very down to earth. He didn't have any of this aura of entitlement that unfortunately comes with a lot of the amateur players that are getting attention from scouts have.

"He obviously knew that he hadn't really established much of a track record as a hitter and he clearly wanted to hit, even though his arm was beginning to get better and I think they were going to work him back into the rotation at some point that year. I really enjoyed the conversation. I didn't really think anything of it at the time. I just knew he was a little bit different and separated himself in terms of the way he carried himself and how easily the conversation flowed between he and I that day."

Blackmon's recollection of their interactions was a bit more cloudy.

"I don't even remember really meeting Alan Matthews ahead of time," Blackmon said.

Before you begin to think that Blackmon was starting to develop some of that big league attitude Matthews said he didn't detect, his lack of memory of that meeting likely had more to do with his having no realization at the time about what was about to transpire for him career-wise. When he sat down with Matthews, a first-year area scout, it was one of several such meetings Blackmon and his teammates had, and Blackmon was simply wrapping his head around the possibility of being able to contribute to the Yellow Jackets in any way, with a dream of a pro career not even in the twinkle of his eye yet.

Blackmon didn't waste much time showing that what he did against his teammate Duncan in that first at-bat, and for the remainder of the fall, was no fluke. He picked up three hits in the season opener against Youngstown State in 2008. He drove in the go-ahead run in the final game of that series to help finish off a sweep. And he really never stopped hitting, though it wasn't necessarily an "*Aha*!" moment for Mathews, who recalls seeing him in intrasquad games before the season officially started and thinking he was interesting, but didn't see anything that jumped off the page.

Some of that was because Blackmon didn't exactly have the kind of left-handed swing that makes evaluators fall out of their chairs. Even with all of the success he's had in his Rockies career, it's not one of those picture-perfect, put it in a how-to video, kind of strokes.

"He didn't have a great swing and he didn't take a good batting practice and to this day he still doesn't," Matthews said. "He is a game hitter who has tremendous bat-to-ball skills, a tremendous understanding of what the pitcher is trying to do to him and how to hunt the right pitch in the right zone and not miss it because he's got tremendous hand-eye coordination and athleticism."

That's the Blackmon we see now, but no one had seen it yet as that 2008 season began in earnest. Scouts give grades to position players on a 20-to-80 scouting scale for hitting, power, speed, arm, and defense. A plus in any category would be a 60 (or 6) or better, an average grade is a 50.

"He certainly didn't take a batting practice those first few intrasquads that I saw in 2008 that said holy cow this is a big leaguer, this is a top two-round pick," Matthews said. "He didn't really do anything when you're filling out your scout card as a first-year area scout that would make you put any big numbers, five or even sixes on your card and say, 'Oh my gosh this is the guy, this is the dude.' He just was sort of was a steady player. You kind of walked away thinking he was a nice college player that maybe had a chance to be a decent draft as a left-handed hitting extra outfielder. I certainly fell into that bucket. I'm not sure if other people realized his stardom immediately but they didn't bring it to my attention."

To his credit, Matthews did stay on Blackmon, helped of course by the need to see the other players with Georgia Tech, not to mention the high-level opponents that would come in ACC play. As Blackmon continued to rake, the rookie scout realized there might be more there than initially met the eye.

"It was definitely a gradual progression," Matthews said. "One of those guys [where] the more you saw him, the more you appreciated how good he was. Then you would have a conversation with one of his teammates or a former Georgia Tech player that was around the program or an assistant coach and you would get all these anecdotes about his athleticism or his work ethic or things he had done with teammates.

"You just started to kind of put the puzzle together and realize this guy was a little bit different than a lot of the players on the field he was playing with and against and a lot different than the players that would be drafted ahead of him. As far as how he climbed the ladder up the draft board that was definitely a Rockies process and not something where Alan Matthews raised the flag and banged the table and said, 'Guys we have to take this dude with the 79th pick in the draft.'"

Matthews' role in this was far from done, but he is right that how Blackmon ended up going in the second round had more to do with his superiors than any report he gave. The then-rookie scout certainly deserves credit for recognizing that Blackmon had some ability. Without his recommendation, those higher-ups wouldn't have even known to come check out the Georgia Tech outfielder.

Here's how the line of communication typically works: An area scout will build a follow list over the summer and during the fall, players in his or her area they want to at least check out once during the following spring season leading up to that year's draft. When they see a player, they'll file a report, and will reach out to the cross-checkers in the organization. There are regional cross-checkers spread out across the country, with national cross-checkers above them. If those folks corroborate an area scout's evaluation, that will often lead to a scouting director visit to see a player and, if that player is being considered with a top pick, then even the general manager might show up.

Matthews had Blackmon and others from that Yellow Jackets team on his follow list and when Blackmon started out the 2008 season hitting, he filed positive reports, even if they weren't "bang the table for a second-rounder" ones. He wanted those above him to check out this first-year hitter.

Danny Montgomery had 10 years as an area scout under his belt, two with the Dodgers starting in 1990, the rest with the Rockies, the only other organization he's worked for since. By 2008, he was a national cross-checker for Colorado, well-respected and with a ton of contacts in the game. One of those connections, with Coach Hall at Georgia Tech, would prove to be a huge advantage.

By the time Montgomery was able to make his way to Atlanta to see Georgia Tech, Blackmon had established himself as one of the best college hitters in one of the best conferences in the country, albeit with virtually no track record of success. Montgomery, known throughout the industry as D-Mont, flew across the country in May of that year from California to see what Blackmon was all about on a Sunday. And, by Montgomery's account, he did Charlie Blackmon like things, hitting the ball hard and running well.

"I was like, wow he is running 4.0," Montgomery recalled. "I went back and looked at my reports and I was like wow this guy has some kind of speed. He was short to the ball, could drive the ball to the opposite gaps. He could do a lot of things as an athlete and I was like wow, where did this guy come from?"

Scouts who have been in the business a while tend to develop a sense and will often have a gut feel about a player. But because

Blackmon hadn't been on many radar screens as a hitter, it wasn't a long enough look for Montgomery to know for sure that he was looking at a future big leaguer.

This is when that connection with Coach Hall came in handy. D-Mont and Hall spent a lot of time after that Sunday game talking, largely about Blackmon. Hall assured his longtime friend that what he saw was no fluke. Blackmon, after all, would end up hitting .396/.469/.564 with 25 steals for the Yellow Jackets in 2008, hitting in all but seven of his 62 games and never going more than one game without a hit. Montgomery thought Blackmon might have the ability to play center field, but was playing a corner in deference to Jeff Rowland, a more experienced outfielder who would go on to play a couple of years in the Tigers organization. Hall agreed Blackmon might have that skillset, and also tipped Montgomery off to a makeup game the next day on Monday, not a typical gameday on the college schedule.

"And again it goes back to the relationships you have with people you trust," Montgomery said. "When you've been in this game so long you have coaches and assistant coaches that you really trust their word even though you know your last word is going to come from your area guy. But I trusted Danny with everything that he had said."

This is where the story picks up a little bit of an espionage feel to it, and that's not uncommon in the world of scouting. The best evaluators in the game will often keep things close to the vest, lest their competitors find out how much they like a guy. So, Montgomery stuck around an extra day and told no one, not even his area scout, Matthews, who thought his cross-checker had gone home to Charlotte after a long trip out west. D-Mont wanted no one to know he was going to watch Blackmon again, hoping to keep him as off the radar as possible.

He wouldn't be alone. Rolando Pino, then a Florida-based area scout for the Cubs, was on a swing to see the top players in

Georgia. He, too, knew about the makeup game and thought he'd have the place to himself. Now the co-director of international scouting for the Boston Red Sox, Pino recalls arriving only to see a familiar face.

"I didn't think anybody would be coming up on a Monday. Sure enough, D-Mont was there."

Montgomery saw Pino as well, but the two acted as if the other didn't exist, not talking, not acknowledging each other, sitting at opposite ends of the ballpark to attract as little attention as possible. But it wasn't until very recently that Montgomery learned the identity of that lone scout with him that day.

"I knew there was another scout at the game. He was sitting way up in the corner," Montgomery said. "Just doing pretty much what I was doing, trying to stay discreet but he was there and he did not tell me that until [a recent trip to the] Dominican that he is still upset at me every time he sees me that he should have gotten that kid because he went back and saw him the next day also."

"It was a good day," Pino said. "I thought Charlie was an everyday player in the second round; that's how I put him in."

Montgomery was on the same page, liking Blackmon more than Matthews did, who saw him more as a third-to-fifth rounder.

"Obviously, had they listened to my recommendation this guy would have been in a uniform and making All-Star Games for another organization," Matthews said.

While Montgomery's opinion carried a lot of weight in the Rockies' draft room, he still had to get decision-makers on board with his opinion. And since he didn't see Blackmon until mid-May, time was running out to make that happen, with ACC Tournament play and then the NCAA postseason coming after that. Georgia Tech did play in a Regional, but given that first round takes place right before the draft, (in 2008, the draft started on June 5; Georgia Tech's season came to an end with a

Regional loss to Georgia on June 2), the only real opportunity to get scouting director Bill Schmidt and assistant general manager Bill Geivett in would be the ACC Conference Tournament in Jacksonville, Florida, just days after Montgomery saw Blackmon for the first time.

By this point, Schmidt had seen the solid reports from his first-year area scout and then was being told by his veteran cross-checker he had to find the time to see this outfielder from Georgia Tech. Schmidt had been the Rockies' scouting director since 1999, becoming the vice president of scouting just one year prior, in 2007, a job he held until he became interim general manager in May 2021. There are only so many days on the scouting calendar and those conference tournaments are often the last trips a director will make before settling into the draft room to prepare for that year's draft.

"I told him when you go into that tournament there is just one guy I want you to pay attention to and just keep it quiet as you can because I'm going to push Billy to get this guy way higher than he probably wants to take him," Montgomery said.

Also by this point, Schmidt had learned to listen when Danny Montgomery spoke. So when he said he had to check Blackmon out, he headed to the ACC Tournament. The beauty of going to a college conference tournament is you can see a whole lot of talent at one time, so Schmidt knew that by checking in on Blackmon, he'd get one last look at future first rounders like Buster Posey, Yonder Alonso, Jemile Weeks, and Allen Dykstra, all of whom went before the Rockies made their first pick at No. 25 overall in the first round, not to mention scores of other potential draftees.

Blackmon didn't disappoint, going 8-for-13 with six runs scored and five runs batted in over three games. It's obviously not just numbers that scouts look at; otherwise, they wouldn't bother going to the games. But Schmidt liked what he saw right from the get-go.

"I could see what Danny was so excited about," Schmidt recalled. "Charlie at that time was probably a 70 runner. I liked the swing, he was fluid, there was bat speed. You look from a tool standpoint, he was a tall rangy kid. Yeah, he didn't have a lot of history, so you start asking questions."

No scouting director is going to take a player as high as the second round on a hunch or based on one good look. And as much as the Rockies liked the work Matthews had put in, he was a rookie and hadn't established his bona fides just yet. So, Schmidt relied on the longer-standing relationships he had, with his cross-checker, with Blackmon's coach and the rapport between those two.

"This game is about relationships and people you can trust that are going to lead you the right way. The two Dannies [Montgomery and Hall], I respect both of them. There's a lot of trust with both and I had a history with Danny Hall back before I got to Colorado. So when Danny Hall signed off on the makeup and the workouts and all of that.... You want to know if you are late to the party and everybody else already knew about him and you're getting in there late, but that wasn't the case."

Schmidt felt Blackmon wasn't just a college performer, but one who had loud tools that would fit in center field, his opinion lining up nicely with Montgomery's. That, along with Allan Matthews' positive reports on Blackmon's play and character, had the Rockies very interested in bringing Blackmon into the fold. The only question would be when.

The Rockies brain trust, those who would be most responsible for answering that question and lining up the draft board, had been together for a while. Dan O'Dowd, now an analyst for MLB Network, had taken over as the club's general manager in September 1999. He came from the Cleveland Indians and brought Schmidt with him. This 2008 Draft would be their

ninth together in Colorado. It was not their first rodeo. O'Dowd
explains:

> We spent a lot of time defining what we liked in
> players and making sure everybody spoke the same
> language. Even though Alan was a young scout, he had
> a great maturity about him and a feel and he asked
> good questions. D-Mont spent a lot of time with
> him that year, too. So he did a lot of great back-
> ground work on Charlie and we always asked the
> question, 'Why do you like him?' Alan really was able
> to elaborate how he felt Charlie got to be the player
> that we all felt he was. That was the job of the area
> scout. The game is about relationships and nobody
> is better at creating and making relationships than
> D-Mont. As you know he is great at that. You know
> he is a great compliment to Billy in that way and so
> his relationship to college coaches is really important.
> It allows you to get greater insight into players and
> allows you to make good picks. Organizations who
> have great relationships with college programs and
> even high school programs are going to make better
> selections with players than organizations who simply
> put no value into that at all.

Having the relationships and liking a player are one thing.
Having the... intestinal fortitude... to take that player in the
second round after just one year of competitive play is quite
another. Thanks to their work, the Rockies had a sense that few
teams liked Blackmon as much as they did. Or at least as much
as Montgomery did, who really pushed for him in the second
round. That's where Pino, the Cubs' area scout who was at that
makeup game, had put him in his report, though the Rockies

didn't know that at the time. Chicago picked No. 65 in the second round that year, the Rockies had pick No. 72.

The Cubs took Wichita State right-handed pitcher Aaron Shafer with that second-round selection; one hurdle cleared. The second obstacle might have been the Rockies' own draft board. Scouting staffs have to be prepared for all sorts of possibilities and outcomes, so it's not like Blackmon was the only name on their board for the second round. After taking a college pitcher, lefty Christian Friedrich, in the first round, they were leaning college bat for that second pick. And right next to Blackmon's name—ahead of it, as some tell it—was South Carolina infielder James Darnell.

It was a different profile, for sure, with Darnell a power-hitting corner infielder who had mashed 19 homers that spring (and 19 the year prior) and Blackmon a speedy outfielder with a better feel to hit, but the lighter résumé. Had both been on the board when it was the Rockies' turn, what would have happened... well, that depends on who you ask.

"Hopefully we'll get Charlie in the next round," Schmidt said.

"You know, we may have [taken Darnell]," said O'Dowd. "Danny Montgomery was really pushing hard for Charlie though. I still think at the end of the day we would have taken a pure bat over more of the power projection. Who knows?"

"You really never know," Montgomery said. "When I sat in there with Billy, Charlie was my guy. Going into the draft, sometimes you just pick one guy you have a gut feel for. And you pray that it's going to work out because in our business you're wrong more than you're right, but you got to at least have some feel of being right more than you're wrong. And sometimes I think that's what I try to hang my hat on, giving Billy all the information, going through all the checks and balances with the area scouts to see if this is our guy. Especially when you are talking about money rounds like in the second round and the lack of history of a guy we want to take in that area. You really have to have a lot of conviction as to what you want out of that guy. Some of it is luck and some of it you really need to have your i's dotted and t's crossed and it worked out for Charlie."

It worked out, at least partially, because the San Diego Padres took Darnell three picks in front of the Rockies, leaving Blackmon as their guy. For his part, Blackmon wasn't even really focusing on the draft yet. He certainly didn't view himself as a second rounder and was kind of using Miami's Blake Tekotte, a fellow ACC outfielder as a measuring stick. Tekotte was a second-team All-American that year, hitting .353 with 13 homers and 27 steals and Blackmon figured once Tekotte went, then he might hear his name called.

"I remember he was one of the better outfielders from Miami and I knew he had been doing it a while and I would kind of wait until he got drafted and I would start paying attention and we kind of flip flopped each other. It was a huge surprise. The second round was way earlier than I thought I'd need to pay attention."

Tekotte would go in the third round, to the Padres. He would get a total of 80 at-bats in the big leagues. Darnell got 62. Both are out of baseball. Blackmon, meanwhile, had more than 5,300 after the 2022 season concluded.

————

Most people think that once a player get drafted and signed and enters a team's player development system, then that ends the connection between the player and the scouts who evaluated him. But while it then is up to the player, along with coaches and instructors, to get to the big leagues, the amateur scouts stay invested.

That summer of 2008, while Blackmon was dipping his toes in professional waters for the first time, Alan Matthews was poring over box scores and streaming audio of the Tri-City Dust Devils, Blackmon's team in the short-season Northwest League clear across the country. He hung on every at-bat and Blackmon did not disappoint, hitting .338 to finish second in the league's batting race.

Montgomery never got the chance to spend any time with Blackmon leading up to the Draft beyond watching him play those two games. It's an occupational hazard as a crosschecker. As much as guys like D-Mont rely on relationships, they're never in one place long enough to develop them with the players they're evaluating. So, it wasn't until the following Spring Training, Blackmon's first, that Montgomery really got to see what made Blackmon tick, why his area scout and the Georgia Tech coach spoke glowingly about the outfielder's makeup.

"I know him so well now," Montgomery said. "I don't get up close to them as much until usually when we get them and then I realize how much of an IQ these guys have and how intelligent they are and how much baseball savvy they have, with their abilities to adjust and things like that. Once you get a guy and you talk to them and you're at Spring Training with them and you're around them in the clubhouse, you are like, 'Wow, I think we got something here!' And that happens to me a lot.

"Once we found out what this guy was all about IQ-wise, we had something and you see he's been able to make adjustments and you could have never told me from doing my report he would have had the power that he's had. It's unbelievable what he's been able to do. That's why I said it's not an exact kind of science here."

It took a while for the power to show up; those around the game will tell you it's often the last tool to come as young players add "man strength." Blackmon hit nine homers in his first full season of pro ball, 11 in his second. Even when he made his major league debut in 2011, he was a hit-over-power type, one who hit .308 in the minors but only had 39 homers in 1,979 at-bats before establishing himself as an everyday big leaguer. Even those who liked him could not have predicted he would turn into an All-Star several times over, a multiple Silver Slugger Award winner. A batting title that he won in 2017? Okay, maybe that's believable. But a thumper who would average nearly 32 homers per season over four years from 2016–2019? No way, no how, but all tip their cap to Blackmon's work ethic and his smarts, giving him all the credit for making the most of every opportunity he's been given, starting back when Rusty Greer thought he might be able to play the outfield a little bit.

"I have said this before and I will say it again—by no means do I take credit for Charlie Blackmon's career or anything he's done," Greer said. "That is all on Charlie. Charlie was, and still is, one of the hardest workers, and is an 'I will do anything you want me to' guy."

"I don't think anybody could have predicted this guy could be an All-Star and be one of the better hitters in the game for many years," Danny Hall said. "I don't think anybody saw that. I certainly didn't. Did I think he could play in the big leagues? Yes I did, but not at the level he's been able to play at. In saying that, one of the things I don't think a lot of people realize is he was an academic All-American; he's really smart. He has become a student of hitting. He's always been a hard worker."

"It comes back to his work ethic, his drive," Schmidt said. "Again, I knew he had tools. Did I ever think he was capable of hitting 30-plus home runs a year? No. It really comes down to what's inside the package. I always use that term to our guys. As much as you try to know what makes them tick and what drives them, I would say that the biggest thing with Charlie is his desire to be great."

A combination of a desire to excel, a confidence in one's ability to maximize the talent they have, and the humility to understand just how hard it is to do that is rare indeed. Blackmon has the ability to look back while he's still doing his thing, understanding that his winding path is perhaps what defines and drives him the most.

"I think it helps me keep things into perspective. Baseball is just so hard and there is so much failure. And I had lots and lots of failure and without that I don't think I would have been able to make the jump from level to level. You know there were so many times when I thought I was done. This is the injury, or this bad performance. I just felt like baseball was going to get taken away from me and then I got another chance. It seemed like that every step of the way.

"I think my perspective has changed a little bit and now I kind of look around the league a little bit and I like to find players who remind me how hard the game is. I like to see guys who struggle, make adjustments, and then become competitive and then succeed. It's very cyclical and more so than any other sport and I think the beauty of baseball is it's so developmental. You cannot translate an amateur talent directly into the big leagues. It just can't be done you know. It's not like the NFL or basketball where bigger, stronger, faster plays. Baseball is all about baseball skills and development of those skills and how you use your mind to let those skills show through. That is why it's so hard, that's why we had 50 rounds in the draft. You just don't know who is going to out-develop everybody else. I mean it helps to start with tools and talent and that kind of thing but there are always those surprises in every draft class that overachieve."

Chapter 6

Ian Kinsler

Every stop of Ian Kinsler's amateur career, the chip on his shoulder that would drive him was given the opportunity to grow.

Even though he was drafted a total of three times as an amateur, wherever Ian Kinsler played, there was always someone who was perceived to be a better player.

He was too small; chip grew. He wasn't strong enough; chip grew.

He played with a future first-round pick in high school, but while he ended up being a late-round pick his senior year, he was barely recruited by colleges.

And the chip grew.

He was one of three future big leaguers on his junior college team the following year and one of five players drafted who were on the roster. But he only improved his draft stock slightly (selected by the same organization both times). The chip grew more.

He took advantage of his strong season to go play for an in-state, four-year school, a Division I powerhouse. Once there, he lost his job to a future major league All-Star and World Series champion, forcing him to be on the move once again. Enormous chance for the chip to grow.

After his final collegiate stop, he finally started his pro career, but not before two of his teammates were drafted ahead of him (that team also had two top-five-round picks the following year). More chip.

That chip, that desire to prove people wrong, was a huge factor in his 14-year major league career that included four All-Star nods, nearly 2,000 hits, more than 250 homers, and over 240 stolen bases. Kinsler would finish with a career WAR of 54.1, more than his high school teammate, more than any of his junior college teammates, even more than the star who took his job.

––––––––

Canyon del Oro High School sits in the Oro Valley of Arizona, right outside of Tucson. It typically has around 1,600 students and has a pretty strong baseball history, with nine players getting drafted from the program and a total 14 alumni playing pro ball over the years.

Its heyday was right around when Kinsler roamed the halls, and the infield, of the school. In 1998, Shelley Duncan graduated from Canyon del Oro and would go on to be an All-American at nearby University of Arizona, en route to being a second-round pick of the Yankees in 2001. The Class of 1999 had two players selected in that June's MLB Draft, with Shelley's brother, the late Chris Duncan, becoming the highest-ever draftee when he went No. 46 overall to the St. Louis Cardinals. His teammate Scott Hairston, who had moved from Illinois for his senior year, went in the 18th round before going on to Central Arizona College, a path that will come into play in Kinsler's story as well.

In 2000, Kinsler's senior year of high school, there were two other star attractions. One was Ryan Schroyer, who would be taken in the 16th round that June and then go on to play at Arizona State and San Diego State before joining the Red Sox as a fifth-rounder in 2004. He had a legitimate power arm with a relief profile, but injuries kept him from getting very far and he spent three years in the minor leagues.

The other was Kinsler's best friend, Brian Anderson, an intriguing two-way prospect who a lot of teams liked as a pitcher. Anderson also had a very strong commitment to attend Arizona. There were teams interested, for sure, though it was unclear whether they could sign him away from his desire to play for the Wildcats the following year.

Often, when a player like Anderson has a solid college commitment, that player will either tell teams not to draft him or let teams know how large of a bonus would be needed to keep him from heading to school. Whether that happened with Anderson isn't germane to this story, but folks in and around the Canyon del Oro baseball program did think he had the chance to get drafted.

Kinsler was excited for his friend and teammate's future, whatever it might be, as the draft approached. So they got together on draft day to tune in. Back in 2000, that meant going to MLB. com and listening to the conference call; baseball's draft wouldn't be officially televised until 2007. They waited.

And waited.

"We're sitting there watching the draft on our dial-up computer," Kinsler said. "And listening to it, thinking Brian's probably going to get picked in the top 10 rounds. His name never got called on the first day, which I guess wasn't unexpected."

Kinsler had done a few showcases and workouts but had no expectations that June whatsoever. He was an athletic and heady infielder who lacked strength and hadn't even been recruited by any college programs. So draft time was all about celebrating with Anderson. In the end, though, he wasn't the CDO player in the room taken.

"We thought there was a chance," Kinsler said, talking about Anderson's prospects. "And then on the second day, we were listening, just kind of hanging around and next thing you know, my name gets called. And I get a call from the Diamondbacks, picking me in 29th round. So it was a really unusual experience."

Anderson never heard his name called during the 2000 Draft. But he did go on to play for Arizona, turn himself into a premium athlete, and get drafted by the White Sox in the first round of the 2003 Draft, making it to the big leagues as an outfielder. He played parts of five seasons in the big leagues, mostly with Chicago. He did go back to the mound to try to recreate himself as a pitcher in 2010 and 2011, but his last major league game came at the end of the 2009 season as an outfielder with the Red Sox.

Kinsler had absolutely no inkling that any team would draft him that year, or that any scout had any interest. Sure, scouts were around the program all the time over the years and Schroyer and Anderson brought them in for the 2000 season. But surely no one was paying attention to Kinsler, who by his own admission was six-foot and maybe 165 pounds at the time.

But Louie Medina was. Kinsler was never the focal point, obviously, but the D-backs area scout in Arizona at the time was drawn to him, seeing him repeatedly as he made multiple trips to Tucson to check in on Schroyer and Anderson.

"That was the best high school team I've ever seen, and there isn't a close second," said Medina, whose last year as an area scout came in that 2000 season before moving to the pro side with the Kansas City Royals, the organization he's been with since. "Ian was obviously a good athlete. He had good footwork and really good hand-eye, bat-to-ball skills. He just wasn't very strong and didn't hit the ball with authority."

This wasn't just a courtesy pick. Medina wanted to sign Kinsler, knowing it would take some time for him to physically mature and develop. The D-backs were interested in using the draft-and-follow, a mechanism used back then for high school players who weren't quite ready. In those days, a team had control over a drafted player until the following May, right before the next draft, if he didn't go to a four-year school. The player would go to a junior college and the team would monitor his progress. If they saw fit, they would then try to sign the player before the deadline. (Spoiler alert: A draft-and-follow pitcher who played with Kinsler in junior college is a big reason why he landed with the team he reached the big leagues with.)

There could have been a chance Kinsler would have been a good candidate for this. He drew zero four-year school offers. Until very late in the game, Kinsler was planning on going to Pima Community College in Tucson, his only real option at the time. Right before the deadline to decide, Central Arizona, one of the better JUCO programs in the country, came to CDO and persuaded Kinsler to join Hairston there.

Two things got in the way of Medina getting his guy. One was money. Medina recalls Arizona not having much left in their draft budget that year to make a solid offer if that had even come to pass. The other was Kinsler's father, Howard.

"His dad was really adamant that his best days were ahead of him, that he was going to get stronger," Medina said. "Every father in every home visit says that. But he deserves credit. Credit goes to Ian for his work ethic, and he believed in himself. But so did his dad."

"Just having the conversation and knowing that I could go to Central and get better, bigger, and stronger, maybe refine my game a little bit… the idea of signing was always, I think, a little bit of an ego massage," Kinsler said. "But I don't know if it was ever realistic. Knowing now what I know, I wasn't anywhere close to being ready to go to an organization and Spring Training… seeing these guys that have been in the minor leagues for two or three years and were a lot bigger and stronger and further along developmentally than I was, it was the right decision. But we definitely had some conversations. It was a fun time to think of the possibilities, but that was really it."

Medina, for his part, tries not to think about what might have been. But he can quietly carry around some bragging rights.

"I haven't talked to Ian since then, but privately, silently, I was really proud of him," Medina said. "I don't want to say I was the only one who liked him, but I believe I was the guy who was on him the most in high school. Other scouts may have liked him, but their team didn't take him. But nobody thought he was going to hit like he did."

———

Kinsler brought his bat-to-ball skills and his feel for the game with him to Central Arizona for the 2001 season. To give you an idea of just how successful a program this has been in producing players, Baseball-Reference lists 124 players to have gone from playing for the Vaqueros to having some kind of professional career through the 2022 season, with 159 players drafted over the years. Before Kinsler, the biggest product to come from the JUCO program was probably reliever Doug Jones, a 1978 January draftee. (Yes, they used to have multiple drafts back in the day, and Jones was a third-round selection in what was known as the January Draft-Regular Phase.) Jones would go on to find fame, and make five All-Star teams, as a big league closer, finishing with 303 career saves.

When Kinsler arrived in 2001, the Vaqueros were already used to winning. A lot. They were ACCAC Conference Tournament champions in 1999 and won the conference's regular season title the following year. It's a trend that continues to this day. Central Arizona won the NJCAA College World Series in 2022, its second title in three seasons, and it's won four total (1976, 2002).

Kinsler headed to campus still under the control of the D-backs for that spring and the organization had the ability to negotiate with Kinsler, as a draft-and-follow, all spring. There were some talks between the Kinsler family and the D-backs regarding trying to get something done, but it never got to the point of anything truly serious.

"I don't remember what the number was, but I honestly wasn't ready, just in terms of maturity, and it made me a little nervous just thinking about going to play minor league baseball at the time," Kinsler said. "I knew I wasn't ready so I honestly didn't pay attention much to the conversations that were happening."

It didn't affect his play much. If Kinsler, as a 19-year-old infielder playing on a stacked JUCO team with a major league organization tracking him, was anxious at all about that kind of pressure, he didn't show it. He would finish third on the team with his .403 average (one of 39 players at the NJCAA Division I level in the country to hit over .400 that year) and would land in the top 20 in the nation with his 22 stolen bases.

"I got better baseball-wise and my instincts got better, but size-wise, my physicality still wasn't quite there," Kinsler said.

Kinsler re-entered the draft after things didn't work out with the D-backs. He would be one of five players selected in the 2001 Draft from the program. While it certainly didn't hurt Kinsler's confidence to be named second-team All-Conference and be mentioned in a group of players like this, it wasn't all that new for him. He had played, after all, with four big leaguers in high school, many of whom he had played with since childhood. While he saw many of them go on to major colleges while he continued to draw moderate interest from scouts and schools, he never once thought he didn't belong.

"I knew we were good and we were the best team in Arizona," he said about his 2001 Central Arizona squad. "But my high school was loaded and we all grew up together. So I was already established at that level. There was already that competitive relationship going on with baseball and my teammates. Going to Central was just another little level up.

"I just wanted to be the best on the team. And I think that's pretty much reflective of my whole baseball career. Not selfishly, I just wanted to be the guy that people depended on."

Central Arizona did depend on him to play shortstop. Ironically, back in high school, Kinsler had played second base in deference to Hairston, who was a year ahead of him. When Hairston left for his first season at Central, Kinsler moved back to his natural spot on the left side of the infield. By the time he reunited with Hairston in 2001, he stuck at short and it was Hairston playing second base.

"I had no problem moving to second base," said Hairston, who would go on to spend parts of 11 seasons in the big leagues, and now provides hitting instruction for young players in Arizona. "He was a better shortstop than I was at that time. There wasn't any pushback whatsoever. I was just happy he was there and I was familiar with playing with him. It was really cool."

They were different players, albeit on the same path, and Kinsler readily admits that Hairston's bat was way ahead of his at the time. There's a reason why Hairston would be the first Vaqueros player taken in that 2001 Draft, a third-round pick of the D-backs.

"Junior college is also a very good place to develop and show your skills, especially here in Arizona," said Hairston, who fully understood the growing chip on Kinsler's shoulder. "You don't have to go to a university to prove you can be a professional player or a big league player. That's what we were out to prove, and we did that."

Medina had moved on to the Royals by then, so it wasn't a matter of a scout being familiar with players he had evaluated in high school. This time it was Steve Kmetko, now a scout with the Yankees, who had the area. Arizona spent a lot of time watching Hairston, so Kmetko got plenty of looks at Kinsler all spring with several of his colleagues in the organization. Hairston would sign with the D-backs, but Kinsler improved his draft spot by just three rounds, not enough to convince him that now was the time to sign.

"I moved up three rounds, to the same team," Kinsler chuckled. "In hindsight, I obviously made the correct decision. I feel like the first conversations out of high school were a lot more exciting than the second."

Back to that spoiler alert for a minute. That Central Arizona team had a very deep pitching staff in 2001, but the one who had the most interest in terms of a future big league career was Rich Harden. Like Kinsler, Harden was a draft-and-follow. The A's had taken the right-hander, a Canadian high school standout who had been taken by the Mariners in the 39th round of the 1999 Draft, in Round 17 of the 2000 Draft after his first season at Central Arizona, then watched his progress very carefully in his sophomore season there all spring. As often as was possible, A's scout Ron Hopkins would watch Harden's starts. Oakland would come to terms with Harden and Hopkins stored away his opinion of Kinsler, until it would once again be relevant when he ran the scouting department for the Texas Rangers.

―――――

Kinsler largely put thoughts of the draft and his pro career out of his mind at this point. He didn't realize any of the previous two seasons were in many ways the starting process of him getting to the big leagues. He always had the inner confidence, the belief Medina saw back during his home visit after the 2000 Draft, that he would eventually get drafted and get an opportunity to play pro ball. Maybe because he knew he wasn't ready to make that step at the time, he didn't connect any of the dots that those who saw him at that time would help shape where he would go in the future.

Instead, he focused on summer ball. He headed to the Jayhawks League and suited up for the Liberal Bee Jays in 2001, a team in the Kansas wood-bat league. He'd hit a respectable .280 for Liberal that summer, playing for head coach Jon Wente, who had been Central Arizona's pitching coach and recruiting coordinator... another dot to connect for Kinsler to further his career.

By this point, Kinsler was getting the attention of Division I schools. He received multiple calls and even went on a recruiting visit to Arkansas. Near the end of the summer, he got a call from Arizona State and it became a relatively easy call to stay in-state and head to the perennial power coached by Pat Murphy that had been a top 25 team in 2001 and was expected to be again in 2002 when Kinsler would join the team.

But first, he had to wait. For whatever reason, ASU didn't have a scholarship lined up right away for Kinsler in the fall of 2001. So he was in baseball limbo. He couldn't go to class in Tempe for the fall, so he took classes at Central Arizona. But he wasn't allowed to attend fall practice with the Vaqueros, going to spend time with his soon-to-be Sun Devils teammates and working out with them when he could. It was obviously a far cry from the reps he'd have gotten at the junior college level, where fall practice wasn't regulated like it is in Division I, and he didn't have the daily opportunity to mesh with his new team and develop there.

He was, by his account, behind when the spring began in 2002. Kinsler was slated to be the starting shortstop for the Sun Devils, forming a very strong double-play combination with a freshman who had made a strong first impression. He and Kinsler meshed well up the middle in practice and intrasquad scrimmages. But when it became go time, when ASU was playing host to an opening-season tournament, Kinsler didn't feel ready.

He was able to scratch out some hits early on, going 9-for-30 (.300) in his first eight games. But as had been the case earlier in his amateur career, he wasn't really impacting the ball. He went 0-for-7 in a late-February series against Loyola-Marymount and got taken out for a pinch hitter twice. From there he saw his playing time diminish, often coming in as a substitute or not playing at all. For the year, he ended up with just 61 total at-bats and not much to show for it, finishing with a .232/.246/.262 line. Only two of his 14 hits were for extra-bases.

That freshman second baseman, who also played some third base early on, took his job by mid-March. He turned out to be pretty good himself: Dustin Pedroia would go on to be a sec-ond-round pick in the 2004 Draft and would win a bunch of awards and two World Series with the Red Sox. He and Kinsler were contemporaries in the big leagues, often vying to be the American League's best second baseman. But despite those who would like to spin a fable about a nasty rivalry that started when Pedroia supplanted him at shortstop at ASU, Kinsler puts out that flame in a hurry. The two have always gotten along and still talk semi-regularly to this day.

If you want to get the first real glimpse into what made Kinsler tick, at what allowed him to turn into one of the best second basemen of his generation, this might be it. It obviously wasn't anything he did on the field; he spent more time on the bench than on the dirt in 2002. It's how he handled it and how he somehow turned it into a positive that helps define who he was, and who he would become.

Most people, given this turn of events, would have grown angry, sullen. Many would have started letting doubt creep in. And who could blame him? He was a smallish infielder who had already been somewhat ignored, who was getting his chance to show what he could do at the highest level of college baseball, only to have it taken away after a relatively slow stretch. He's not sure if it was naivete or the blissful ignorance of youth, but he never let the negativity eat at him.

"There are a lot of things that you can say negatively about Arizona State at the time and Pat Murphy and the way things were handled," Kinsler said. "But the flip side of that is that I learned a lot from him. He is a very knowledgeable baseball guy. And he held a lot of team meetings, he talked about the games extensively, on the little moments and what can happen, that from the first pitch on can be a play that changes the outcome of the game."

"I just tried to control what I could and I just tried to learn as much as I could through the rest of the year because I never sat and watched the game. And just listening, learning, watching, working, I worked really hard and practiced constantly, like it never affected me as far as my effort and what I thought of myself as a player."

The chip was flourishing, but it never made him bitter. Though he had been overlooked and pushed aside, he also had been noticed. By Central Arizona. By the D-backs twice. By ASU, even if that had gone south. That helped him realize there was still a greener pasture waiting for him somewhere.

"It had been there since I was a kid and then all these things just continued to grow that chip," Kinsler said. "But the reason I wasn't just like, 'Screw this! This is crap!' and I didn't take that situation negatively was because I had been drafted twice. I had been recruited by other schools, so I knew I was capable of being drafted and it was my sophomore year and I had a year left to prove myself and to get that opportunity again. I was always looking ahead and I was always trying to get better and put myself in a situation to get drafted because really that was the ultimate goal, to give myself an opportunity to see what I could do. If you get negative in a situation like that, then your growth just stops."

Not that Kinsler ever lacked internal motivation, but if he ever did, Mikel Moreno was there to reignite that fire. Moreno had played at Arizona State from 1995 to '98 and was an All-American, one who helped the Sun Devils reach the postseason twice and finish as the runner-up in the 1998 College World Series. After a couple of years of pro ball, Moreno went on to coach in a variety of positions at a variety of schools. He was an assistant at Central Arizona when Kinsler came through and later worked as a graduate student coach at his alma mater.

Moreno is, simply put, intense. He played with a hair-on-fire mentality that made him a favorite among Sun Devils fans. Later on, when he was an assistant, he would have a huge falling out with Pat Murphy over his involvement in calling out Murphy's behaviors and actions as head coach. But in 2002, he was still a beloved ASU alum who was remembered by teammates for threatening anyone who ever said anything bad about the program in a team meeting after the 1998 College World Series run. Suffice it to say, he was an excellent go-between for Kinsler and ASU.

"At that time, I had a really good relationship with Pat Murphy and the coaches," Moreno said. "And early on, I said, 'This is your starting shortstop, you've got to get him,' because I wasn't that far away from playing. And I thought, 'This guy can play at that level.'"

Moreno talked frequently with Kinsler during that spring of 2002 and, because he had played a part in getting him to Tempe, he felt some responsibility when things went sideways for Kinsler. Even in those private conversations, Kinsler never took the low road to rip the program, the coach, or his circumstances.

"He didn't bad mouth anybody," Moreno recalled. "There was no vendetta for him. He might have used it as fuel, but he never used it as an excuse."

He definitely utilized it to work hard that summer. There was a new summer wood-bat league in the Phoenix area that year, and who wouldn't want to play outdoors in Arizona in the summer? The competition level was not up to Kinsler's standards, but he was able to play regularly for the first time in a long while. And he was able to get extra work in with Moreno, while also fielding calls from other Division I programs who were offering the potential to transfer.

Moreno had seen Kinsler's work ethic first-hand at Central Arizona, where he never heard a complaint about a 6:00 AM workout, or extra hitting after a doubleheader. If there was a coach who could push Kinsler too hard, he hasn't been found. And Moreno liked to push, so it was a match made in heaven.

"That's how he worked; Ian was so competitive and so driven to work," Moreno said.

"He was constantly riding me," Kinsler said. "And so after one of those summer league games, he was just hitting me fungo after fungo after fungo. I used to stay behind and take hundreds of ground balls. He would just rifle balls at me."

"Unfortunately for some players, that's just how I coach every day," Moreno said. "It was always pretty intense and Ian kind of thrived in that."

It was during one of those intense summer workouts that Tim Jamieson visited, a trip that would change Kinsler's life forever. At that point, Kinsler was fielding calls from other schools about getting a new opportunity with them. Florida International, Nebraska, and Long Beach State were among the programs expressing interest. That last one intrigued Kinsler because it was a very highly regarded program at the time. None of these schools could guarantee a starting spot, let alone a definite yes to letting him play shortstop. Long Beach State wanted him to come but told him they had a good shortstop coming in, so he'd have to compete for a job elsewhere. Kinsler knew he wanted to play short, and play every day, to give him the best chance to get drafted, and his internal reaction was not a good one.

"My chip is big and I'm thinking, 'Yeah, right. I can beat out anybody. Whatever,'" Kinsler recalled. "Looking back...."

The new shortstop coming in to play for the Dirtbags was Troy Tulowitzki, who would go on to become a first-round pick and make five All-Star teams with the Colorado Rockies.

Jamieson, at the time, was the head coach of the University of Missouri. He had taken the helm there in 1995 and in 1996 helped them win a conference title and head to an NCAA Regional. The Tigers strung together six straight 30-plus win seasons in a row, but in 2002, they stumbled to a 24–29 record. The program needed an infusion of talent, which is why Jamieson headed to Arizona to check in on Kinsler.

He didn't head to the area with no prior knowledge of Kinsler. Jamieson said they lightly recruited him out of high school, though it never got to any kind of offer, which is why it never really landed on Kinsler's radar back then. Mizzou had moved on, but when Jamieson and his staff learned Kinsler was leaving ASU, they figured it couldn't hurt to reach out and see if there was interest. While Kinsler wasn't ready to commit to the transfer just yet, there was enough of a sense of his need to leave Tempe that Jamieson flew in to watch him in that summer league. It was during his defensive work with Moreno that he quickly ascertained Kinsler would be an upgrade.

"I watched him take some ground balls and after like the second ground ball, I said, 'He's better than anybody we have or anybody we've had,'" said Jamieson, now the pitching coach at Memphis. "So it didn't take much of an evaluation to figure out he could help us play, but that all happened pretty quickly."

Jamieson spent another couple days watching Kinsler, though he said that wasn't necessary other than to convince Kinsler to come play for him. While he wouldn't automatically guarantee anything, he made it pretty clear that the shortstop gig was his, and they had the scholarship money to make it happen. Once Kinsler found out the school was in the Big 12 and played "really good baseball schools" like Texas and Oklahoma, he was ready to go… though he didn't know exactly where he was going at the time.

"I had a knack for making decisions without really discussing it," Kinsler said. "It just felt right and I went for it. So I told coach Jamieson I'm going to Missouri. I call my dad and tell him the news. And he asks, 'Okay, where's Missouri?' And I said, 'I have no idea.'

"I didn't even know where Missouri was on the map at the time. It was the center of the United States somewhere. But I was going to Columbia… I had no idea that the University of Missouri was in Columbia, Missouri. I had never heard of the city or where the state was. I knew I was playing shortstop in the Big 12 and that's all that mattered."

———

Many people think all the work done by scouts happens during the spring. That is, after all, when baseball season is, so it makes some sense. Games start, scouts go see games, rinse and repeat. It's far from that simple.

Scouts might start to build their follow lists for the spring the previous summer at leagues and showcases, but there's also a ton of work done in the fall, especially at the college level. Schools have practices, intrasquad games and workouts that scouts can attend. It might help an area scout prioritize who to see in the spring and it often affords time for them to talk to the players and get to know them, with their makeup and character becoming more and more important given the dollars handed to them, especially the top guys.

The vast majority of scouts in Missouri had no idea who Ian Kinsler was, so the fall would be the first time they laid eyes on the transfer. That was not the case for Mike Grouse.

Grouse became the Rangers' area scout in the region back in 1990, so by the time Kinsler came around, he knew the area better than anyone. And while he didn't know Kinsler well, he had seen him play summer ball with the Liberal Bee Jays in the NBC (National Baseball Congress) World Series in Wichita back in the summer of 2001.

"Did I think he was going to be a 30-30 guy? No," said Grouse, who went from being area scout to regional crosschecker and up to being a national crosschecker before switching over to pro scouting, referring to the fact that Kinsler would twice hit 30 homers and steal 30 bases in one big league season. "He was a baseball player. He could run. He was instinctual. He was a leader. He was vocal. He was focused. He was intent."

When Kinsler came in, Mizzou hadn't been to a Regional for five years running. Though he had just arrived, Grouse recalled, he made it clear that's exactly where they would head that spring, solidifying his leadership and winning attitude bona fides. Grouse's long-standing relationship with Missouri's coaching staff helped him gain that insight and it's unclear if other scouts understood that much about what made Kinsler tick.

They did get to see how he competed for much of the fall. Jamieson knew he could defend, and that's why he brought him to Columbia. In what amounted to Kinsler's first prolonged time away from Arizona, other than that summer ball stint, the Tigers' head coach couldn't help but be impressed with how his new player adjusted to the environment.

"We didn't really know much about his bat and didn't really care much about his bat, to be honest," Jamieson said. "As the fall went on, we learned more and more about him as a person and as a competitor and about his hitting skills. Our fall is pretty cold and our biggest concern any time we recruited a guy from the West or South is can they handle our weather when it gets crappy? And one of the first things that impressed me was he didn't bat an eye when it got cold. It didn't affect his game, he didn't complain, and that was kind of the first sign that this guy's a pretty good competitor."

Another sign was that he tried to play through an injury. Kinsler suffered a stress fracture in his foot during a fall scrimmage. He managed not to miss too much time, but it certainly impacted one of his best tools at the time, his speed, and likely hurt his range at shortstop. New to the area, there was no doubt frustration that he couldn't show the best version of himself to the area scouts who had no history with him. Grouse, though, knew what he could do and saw the injury as an advantage to his own scouting.

"At the time, he was more of a defensive player who could handle the bat," Grouse said. "He could handle the barrel and hit the ball to right-center as well as anybody. He just knew how to play baseball and he could run. But the problem was that stress fracture in his foot. The new scouts who had never seen him before didn't know he could run and I sure as heck wasn't going to tell."

Even with the injury, Kinsler went on to hit .335 with six homers and 45 RBIs and even managed to go 16-for-17 in stolen base attempts. He was named the second-team All-Big 12 Conference shortstop, even though he still thinks he was the best player at the position in the conference that year. He made good on the guarantee that the Tigers would head to postseason play, the first of what would be seven straight NCAA Tournament appearances for the program.

It's a large area, the Midwest, with a lot of ground to cover and a lot of players to see. Realistically, Grouse would submit 25 or so players on his list to the organization, a group he admits he would pad to make it seem like he had a really strong area each year. Kinsler was on his list, but certainly wasn't a priority player or high on the list.

Typically, a player ranked like that wouldn't necessarily be seen or known well by the higher-ups. In a conference like the Big 12, Kinsler was going to be seen, but would not have been a point of focus. And for a scouting director coming in to see, say, Baylor outfielder David Murphy, who would be a first-round pick of the Red Sox that June, or Texas' Omar Quintanilla, named the Big-12 first-team shortstop ahead of Kinsler and an eventual supplemental first-rounder of the A's, Kinsler would not have necessarily stood out, especially playing slightly hobbled.

Remember the spoiler alert? This is where the dots of Kinsler's amateur travels connected serendipitously. A quick refresher: In 2001, when Kinsler was at Central Arizona, he was teammates with right-hander Rich Harden. Harden had been taken by the A's in 2000 as a draft-and-follow and sent to pitch in junior college. The A's scouting staff, headed by Grady Fuson, came in frequently to watch Harden pitch. (The A's would sign Harden and he would spend parts of seven seasons pitching in the big leagues for the organization.) It typically was national crosschecker Ron Hopkins who would come to see Harden throw. As a result, "Hoppy," as he is often called, saw Kinsler swing the bat quite a bit in the spring of 2001.

Following that season, the Texas Rangers hired Fuson to be their assistant general manager, a move that actually led to a grievance by the A's and a fine levied against the Rangers because they had interviewed him to be the team's general manager. That had been approved by Oakland, but the organization was not thrilled when Fuson was hired for another post.

Fuson brought Hopkins over from the A's in time to help him run the draft in 2003 and Hopkins would be Texas' scouting director through the 2009 season. He had Grouse's positive reports in hand, along with his own recollection of the 2001 version of Kinsler, when he and Fuson went to the Big 12 Conference Tournament, which often serves as one-stop shopping for scouting directors and executives, a way to see a lot of good players, under playoff-like pressure, at the same time.

"He was the same player in junior college," Hopkins remembered. "Good swing, hard contact, caught the ball, made the plays, could run and throw. It looked like he'd gotten a little bigger, stronger. He had good makeup; he was a baseball player."

Grouse had told him, and Hopkins could clearly see, that Kinsler played with a certain edge.

"He played the game with some passion and energy," Hopkins said. "I like to say he played the game with a chip on his shoulder. He'd been overlooked in the past because of his size, and he played the game that way. And I think that was part of what made him become the player that he was."

Hopkins, and the Rangers, would no doubt add to that chip by waiting until the 17th round to take him. Grouse gets the credit, or blame, depending on which side of the story you're telling, for that.

Because of the amount of time he had served in the area, Grouse had a very good pulse on what went on there and, as Hopkins put it, "knew his competition" among the other scouts. And he understood exactly when they'd be able to get Kinsler. Based on talent, Grouse and the Rangers saw him as a talent who deserved to go anywhere from the fourth to the eighth round.

That's about when Hopkins started asking Grouse about taking Kinsler when the 2003 Draft rolled around in June. But Grouse kept pumping the brakes, kept telling them to wait. Remember the thrilling battle scene in the movie *Braveheart* when William Wallace is leading his Scottish brothers into battle against the British? The British troops are charging and Wallace keeps his soldiers in line by yelling, "Hold!" repeatedly before finally, at the right moment, shouting, "Now!" That was Grouse in the Rangers' draft room, minus the war paint on his face.

Hopkins trusted Grouse, not only in his evaluation of the player, but in his evaluation of the area and his fellow scouts. Heading into the draft, he knew of one other scout who had interest in Kinsler: Mitch Webster. A former big leaguer, Webster was the Midwest scout for the Dodgers at the time and he and Grouse were pretty tight. So Grouse knew that Webster had two shortstops in his sights, Kinsler and a St. Louis–area high school shortstop named Lucas May.

Grouse also knew that if the Dodgers took May, then Webster wouldn't push to take Kinsler because in his experience as a player, he had seen the pattern too many times before, where the college guy comes in and outplays the high school kid, leaving the younger player with no opportunity.

Once Los Angeles took May (who would eventually convert to catching and touch the big leagues briefly in 2010 with the Kansas City Royals) in the eighth round, Grouse could exhale. There was nothing keeping the Rangers from getting Kinsler now and they could wait as long as they needed to take him. The Rangers used that, and the fact that Kinsler was eager to sign and begin his pro career, to their advantage.

Kinsler, of course, knew nothing about what was happening behind the scenes. He didn't know what team or teams were on him or in what round he would get taken. He had interviewed with a few scouts but didn't have a good feel for any of them. The only two things he knew as the draft started was that he wanted to play, to finally prove that he belonged, and that he needed a ride home.

Those two seemingly unrelated thoughts collided that June. Kinsler had arranged to hitch a ride with Jeremy Hernandez, his teammate and double-play partner. Hernandez lived in California and was going to drop Kinsler off in Tucson on the way. The only issue is that Hernandez wanted to leave on the first day of the draft. Columbia to Tucson was at least a 20-hour drive and he was eager to get a move on. Kinsler implored him to wait.

"Dude, we can't drive today," Kinsler recalled telling Hernandez. "Today's the first day of the draft. We need to stay here so we have the internet, so I can see where I get picked. I have to go in the top 10 rounds and I'm thinking we'll just sit through that. We'll hang out in Columbia; we'll listen to the first 10 rounds and then we'll drive."

Believing he was the best shortstop in the conference, he was encouraged when Quintanilla was taken with pick No. 33 overall by the A's. Baylor shortstop Trey Webb was a fifth-round selection of the Montreal Expos. Understanding that he hadn't been seen as much as either of them, he thought he would go in the sixth or seventh round. Two Mizzou teammates, Justin James and Jayce Tingler, went in rounds five and 10, both to the Blue Jays. The first day of the draft went 20 rounds in those days, but when the break in the conference call came after round 10 rounds and Kinsler hadn't heard his name called, Hernandez was ready to hit the road.

Kinsler could feel that chip growing and he begged Hernandez to wait, but to no avail. Given his choices were to go with Hernandez or get stranded, the duo packed up the car and began the journey westward.

They should've waited, since Kinsler did indeed get drafted in that next set of rounds. He did have a cell phone with him, one of those old flip-phone deals, but service was spotty at best on the road, especially back in 2003. No messages were coming in and it might have been the first time Kinsler let some doubt seep into his consciousness.

"Dude, I don't know if I'm going to get drafted, this is crazy," he told Hernandez.

But then when he reached an area with service, his phone blew up, from the Rangers, from family. Fuson and Grouse had called him to tell him he had been selected in the 17th round. Grouse had reached out to Kinsler's father to let him know when he couldn't reach his draftee, and dad was noticeably disappointed he didn't go sooner.

––––––––

Kinsler was beyond eager to start this new chapter, but that chip on his shoulder also told him he should have gone earlier than Round 17, so he went and played back in the Jayhawks League for a spell while negotiating with the Rangers. It wasn't too long of a wait and Kinsler signed and began his pro career that summer, playing solidly over 51 games with Spokane in the short-season Northwest League. After hitting over .400 in the Midwest League in 2005, he double-jumped to Double-A in that first full season and he reached the big leagues in 2006, receiving American League Rookie of the Year votes in the process.

"He did the work, he made himself the player he became," Grouse said. "When we signed him, he and I were sitting at the Chili's at the Kansas City Airport, signing before he had to fly out. And he said, 'You know, I'm going to play in the big leagues.' I said, 'There's no doubt you're going to play in the big leagues.' He had something to prove.

"We took him in the 17th round because that's just the business of it, and that's how it goes. But he knew he was a better player. I think we knew he was a better player."

"That's a big thing in the draft: Anytime you can get a guy later, it enables you to get another good guy higher," Hopkins explained. "I hate to say it, but you get two for one. You get better talent later in the draft and you know once they go out and play…. You may get paid to sign based on your draft, but you get paid in the game based on how you're performing.

"We didn't have any doubt Ian Kinsler would go out and play well and looking back on it, obviously if we were geniuses, he'd have gone a lot higher. You look back at that draft today and come up with a first round, he's a first rounder. There aren't 30 guys that were in that draft who had a career like he did."

At least according to WAR, there wasn't a single player in that draft who signed who had a career like Ian Kinsler did. That 54.1 WAR is 20 higher than the next best player from the class, first-rounder Nick Markakis. His best friend, Brian Anderson, who ended up going No. 15 overall after three years at Arizona, finished with negative WAR. His high school and junior college teammate Scott Hairston? 6.5. Even Dustin Pedroia, with all of his success, finished behind Kinsler at 51.9 after being drafted in 2004.

Perhaps it's not the be-all, end-all, but it's something. Maybe it means that Kinsler can look back at what he willed himself to accomplish with satisfaction? Maybe he can look over that chip on his shoulder and say, "See, I told you I was better than that"?

"Yeah, it does. I can't say that it doesn't," Kinsler said candidly. "But for me, when your career ends and you're done playing baseball, for me personally, those aren't the things I hang my hat on. I hang my hat on the way people portrayed the way I played the game, my effort level, or my intelligence. What feeling did I give them when they watched the game of baseball? That's more important to me than looking back and saying I was the best pick in the 2003 Draft.

"Is it a little notch? Absolutely. And it feels good to say it. But for me, it's more about the everyday grind of baseball and how I tried to play the game."

Chapter 7

Lorenzo Cain

It's the kind of tale that would get you thrown out of any pitch meeting with a Hollywood executive. It would go something like this:

Filmmaker: Our protagonist tries out for his high school basketball team but doesn't make the cut. So he decides to give baseball a try, for the first time in his life, as a sophomore. He plays junior varsity as he tries to catch up with players who have played the game for years. Fast-forward to two years later and he gets drafted by a major league organization. He signs the following spring and then goes on to play more than a dozen years in the big leagues.

Executive: (In between fits of laughter) You've got to be kidding me. Next thing you're going to tell me is that he won a championship or was an All-Star or something ridiculous like that.

Filmmaker: Well, actually, yes. A World Series title, two All-Star appearances, a Gold Glove, an American League Championship Series MVP....

Executive: (Doubling over) Yeah, right. Sorry, this just is so far-fetched, no one would buy it.

Yet this isn't just "based on actual events." The Lorenzo Cain story is 100 percent true.

———————

These days, the top players in any draft class likely started playing baseball at a very early age, beginning with T-ball. (And they often, sadly, specialize in baseball at a pretty young age as well, though perhaps a discussion on the value of maximizing athleticism by playing multiple sports should be tabled for a later time.) Cain was the antithesis of this, having never played a single out of any kind of organized baseball until his sophomore year of high school.

You heard that right.

Not T-ball, not little league, not a pickup game in the park. And if it hadn't been for a fortuitous decision made by the Madison County High School basketball coaching staff—fortuitous to the baseball world anyway—Cain may have never given baseball a try.

Cain didn't have much time for organized sports growing up. After losing his father at a very young age, he made sure he was around as much as possible as his single mother, Patricia, worked two jobs to make ends meet. She wouldn't let him play football in high school (smart move) and the tall and lanky teen thought basketball could be his thing.

Rod Williams and Morris Bell, the Madison County High basketball coaches, thought otherwise. Knowing what we know now, after seeing years of Cain's athleticism on the diamond, scaling walls to rob home runs, and knowing that Madison High had a school population of only around 700 students (Madison, Florida, is a tiny town almost right on the central northern border of Florida, just south of Valdosta, Georgia, Cain's birthplace, and the latest census estimates came in just shy of 3,000 people in the town), it boggles the mind how Cain didn't somehow make that team. But hey, if Michael Jordan could get cut from his high school basketball team, so could Lorenzo Cain. And to their credit, Williams and Bell laugh about and celebrate how that decision worked out for Cain.

At the time, Cain didn't find it funny. Completely dejected, Cain searched for something else to do his sophomore year. He had known Jeremy Haynes since fifth grade. They weren't best friends, but in a town that small, everyone knew everyone and he and Haynes had been in classes together for several years. And Cain knew Haynes was a baseball player, and a good one.

"Everybody was saying, 'Oh, Lorenzo just got cut,'" Haynes said. "I remember seeing him in class that day, and he walked up to me and said, 'Can I play baseball?' I said, 'Yeah, let's go to Coach Myers' office,' because he was the high school coach."

This was not some arrogant high school kid having the audacity to think he could just stroll into the coach's office and onto the field and dominate. Cain was really just looking for something to *do*. Of course, that didn't mean he was going to be handed the center-field job and a spot in the top third of the order like he had for much of his major league career. This was Florida, after all, where baseball is played 365 days a year and high school roster spots are typically tough to come by.

That's what coach Barney Myers had experienced in his decades of high school coaching. A Tampa native, Myers started his coaching career around his hometown in the early 1970s before moving up to the Tallahassee area around 1991. He moved over to Madison County High School as a teacher/football and baseball coach in 2001. So when his life first intersected with Cain's, it was prior to his second year as the Cowboys' coach.

In his previous coaching stops in Florida, there would be try-outs and cuts, more kids than roster spots. But in what turned out to be part two of Lorenzo Cain's serendipity tour, following him not making the basketball team, was that Myers, and Madison County's junior varsity baseball team, desperately needed players.

So when Haynes brought his buddy with him to Myers' office, seeing if Cain could join the program, he was an answer to the veteran coach's prayers.

"Of course, you make the baseball schedule at the start of the year," Myers recalled. "This year, we had 11 kids on our varsity team and we had only eight kids come out for the JV team. But I had put together an entire JV schedule. So I was really nervous.... We had some really good ninth grade players who were going to play on that JV team. They were eventually going to be really good players and they needed to play."

So Myers would tell his varsity team at every turn to be on the lookout for anyone willing to give the JV squad their ninth player. And then that fateful day, soon after Cain found out he would not be fulfilling his basketball dream, Haynes brought him to Myers' office at lunch to see if Cain could sign up. The conversation, according to Myers, went something like this:

Myers: Have you ever played baseball before?

Cain: No sir.

Myers: Little league? T-ball? Nothing?

Cain: No sir.

Myers: But you want to play?

Cain: Yes sir.

Myers: Well, come out there this afternoon. We're practicing and we'll get you going.

How far he'd be going, no one could have any idea, but it's amazing how when one door closed, Cain somehow found another one to walk through.

"I sit back and think, 'Damn,'" Cain told the *Kansas City Star* back in 2014. "One little thing, one change here, one change there, there's no telling where I would have been. If I would have made the basketball team, there's no chance I would have played baseball. I know that for sure. There's no chance."

———————

As the legend of Cain's start in baseball has grown, the mythical nature of it has as well. It's not that the tall tales have exploded into things like him hitting four homers in his first game. Quite the contrary, most of the stories are about just how little he knew about how to play. Most of what's been reported or said is, as advertised at the start of this chapter, wholly accurate. There may be a thing or two that have been added, believed to be canon, but not actually true.

The one main false factoid is about his first time at the plate. The story that has grown is that he got up cross-handed, putting his left hand on top of right as a right-handed hitter. Baseball history buffs will know that Hall of Famer Hank Aaron hit that way as a teenager when he first started out, but myth buster Jeremy Haynes says it's not true, though, "the legend of the story has grown over time."

Don't be too disappointed. The rest of Cain's humble beginnings are still movie-worthy. Myers ran a baseball class for most of the team at the end of the day, seventh period. Cain wasn't a regular part of that class, obviously, since he hadn't been part of the team previously. But he came close to the end of the period to unofficially begin his baseball career.

The myth goes that he showed up in street clothes, and that is absolutely correct. Having never played the sport, he didn't have any gear, so he arrived with basketball shoes, shorts, and a t-shirt. Myers sent him into their makeshift field house to raid the equipment box the team has. Cain found some practice pants and a glove, according to Myers, who sent his new player out to be with the outfielders he had been working with previously.

Myers tried to aim the first fungo hit right at Cain, trying not to challenge him too much. Somewhat awkwardly, Cain made the catch. He then proceeded to take the glove off his right hand and throw the ball back in. Cain had done something not uncommon for someone completely unfamiliar with the game: He had grabbed a glove that fit his dominant hand, and it wasn't until he both saw his new teammates *and* realized that taking his glove off to throw was less than efficient that he recognized a change was needed.

"He says, 'Coach, I can get it in way faster if I had one of those other gloves,'" Myers recalled. "I tell him there are some in there that will go on his other hand. He runs in there and comes out with this baseball glove that had been in the lost and found, one of those plastic gloves, and it had a cut right in the palm of the thing. But it wasn't a leather split. So that was the first glove that he had."

No one could have possibly known Cain would eventually turn his glove from plastic to gold in the big leagues. Not only did he show up that first day without gear, he came with nearly no foundational knowledge of the game. The embellishers would say he didn't know right field from left, first from third. That might be a bit far-fetched, but not too far. He knew no terminology, things like bunting or tagging up were foreign phrases to him. It was a very, very steep learning curve and had this been any other baseball situation, Cain either would have been cut or wouldn't have even tried to come out for the team.

Instead, he became player No. 9 for the Madison County High School junior varsity team. He joined Myers' end-of-the-school-day baseball class to get crash courses on the game. And while Haynes thinks that even if Myers wasn't desperate to fill out a JV roster, Cain would've stuck around, the fact that he *had* to be in the lineup was huge.

"I think being ninth and being able to play every day was a huge part of that first opportunity for him," Haynes said. "He was definitely skinny, but you see a kid like that, with wide shoulders, who could run the way he could run? He always had that ultimate tool you can't teach, that ability to run. You just saw that right out of the gate."

The rest came more slowly. While Haynes was on the varsity team, he saw some of the first very rough early practices and remembers seeing Cain after his first JV game. The varsity would often play right after the JV squad. Cain began playing third base, and it did not go well.

"I walked in the dugout and asked him how it was going," Haynes said. "And he said, 'Man, I have like five errors.' So it was a rough start. But it was literally starting from scratch at 16."

It was on-the-job training for much of that first year, but the combination of the reps and his teammates helped him make some pretty significant strides.

"We had some really good varsity players, like Jeremy Haynes. And we had some players on that JV team who were very good players," Myers said. "So there were some good players for him to emulate and they liked Lorenzo so much, they kind of took him under their wing.

"And he started every game and played every inning of every game that season. He made progress and learned. He learned the entire game from scratch. When he came out, there wasn't a lot of time to teach him things. We just put him out there and he played. He just kept playing and learning."

Myers points to that summer as a key turning point. He would form a summer team with all of the players who would be returning the following year. They played a ton more games and practiced a lot and Cain made huge strides in understanding the game and using his athleticism on the field more consistently.

He had the right mindset to soak it all in. While most teen-agers might feel they know it all, Cain was a sponge who knew he had things to learn. Haynes described him as being quietly competitive, a trait he held throughout his big league career. All he wanted to do was win and excel.

"There were times when he was like, 'I don't know what I'm doing, but I want to be good at it,'" Haynes said.

That led to him taking a lot of extra batting practice and taking a lot of extra balls in the field. And his initial steps forward led to him making the varsity team as a junior. He played a good amount, but not all the time. And that quiet competitiveness took over again. He didn't like not starting every game. So he and the team's Iron Mike pitching machine became best friends. It became the norm for Cain to spend his lunch period with Iron Mike, which you could feed 100 balls into, flip a switch, and take swings.

It was between his junior and senior seasons where things really started to take shape, with all the extra work, the sum-mer games, the tournaments helping Cain improve by leaps and bounds. Haynes remembers seeing glimpses then of who his friend might become, with a huge at-bat here and an astounding catch there, even if it was far from consistent. He had become good enough that when Brewers scout Doug Reynolds called Myers to ask if Haynes, by then a legitimate two-way prospect on scouts' radars, could come to a workout he was holding, Myers asked Reynolds for a favor.

––––––––

Reynolds played his college ball at Liberty University and played three years of pro ball with the Baltimore Orioles, who had taken him in Round 33 of the 1989 Draft. He had been coaxed into scouting by longtime scout Ross Bove after he had quit playing and was coaching junior college ball in Florida. Hired by the Brewers in 1992, it's the only organization he's ever scouted for, serving as an area scout in South Carolina, Georgia, and North Florida until he was promoted to regional crosschecker in November 2008. He is now the national supervisor for Milwaukee's scouting department.

By summer of 2003—the start of Cain's senior year—Reynolds had been working the area for more than a decade. He knew the coaches and the players in the area very well and would annually hold a closed, invite-only tryout camp. Jack Zdurencik was his boss at the time and, as Brewers' scouting director, he loved workouts. So Reynolds gave Myers a call to see if Haynes could come to his planned workout. Myers had no problem with that but then asked Reynolds if he would take a look at someone else as well.

"He says, 'I have another guy. I don't think he's a pro guy. I'm not really sure, it's a unique case. Let me just send him to you and you let me know what you think,'" Reynolds recounted.

"As he kept getting better, I kept thinking that he could play college baseball," Myers said. "This might be a way for him to go to college. It might be a small school, but I bet he can play college baseball at some point. He worked so hard."

Typically, the players Reynolds brought to the summer workout were ones he knew, guys he thought he would bring down to the annual Diamond Club event, usually in October. Reynolds brought a North Florida team down to compete in the tournament that was run by and for scouts. As long as Haynes was there, he figured he might as well take a look at Cain, who he had not seen at all as a junior.

There were maybe 15 players at this workout and one of the first thing Reynolds did was had them all run the 60-yard dash. By this point, Cain had already been working on improving his speed. He had spoken with Myers about what he needed to do to play college baseball and his coach had told him that his ticket was playing the outfield and his potential speed, that he would need to run a good 60. When Cain first started playing, he ran what Myers said was a 60 over seven seconds, not exactly a time that turned heads. So just like Cain would spend his lunch taking swings off the Iron Mike machine, Cain worked to improve his 60-yard time.

"He took that to heart, and he worked at that," Myers said. "He practiced running the 60, he practiced running from home to second. He would practice running and racing people on the football field in the 60-yard dash, because he was told that you have to have a good 60. A lot of what happened to Lorenzo is because he had an amazing 'want to' and work ethic."

That 'want to' helped Cain get much faster and it showed when he ran the 60 for Reynolds.

"Cain, who I don't know who he is, runs I would say, probably a 6.4," Reynolds said. "So I'm already wondering, 'Who is this guy?'"

The next part of the workout was batting practice and Reynolds is very curious to see what Cain can do. Extremely skinny, Cain had a crude swing, something that would take years in the minor leagues to iron out, but even back then some of his innate gifts, like his hand-eye coordination, showed up, albeit inconsistently.

Reynolds fired a pitch and Cain would barely tap it back to the L-screen that protected the scout throwing BP. Then the next Cain swing would deliver a line drive off the scoreboard.

"I'm like, 'What it the world is going on?'" Reynolds said.

The scout called Cain out to the L screen to try to get to know him a bit more. Cain wasn't much of a talker, but it was then Reynolds started to learn about how he had just started playing baseball and that's why he had never seen or heard of him. But Reynolds had seen enough raw ability that he told him he was going to bring him, along with Haynes, to the Diamond Club event, which, of course, Cain had never heard of.

"In fairness, most Panhandle kids don't know what it is," Reynolds said. "It's more or less the All-Star Game in the fall for the state of Florida."

Reynolds picked up Haynes and Cain and drove them down and Reynolds recalls Cain not being overmatched, even picking up a few hits along the way against better competition than he had ever faced. It was then and there the Brewers scout jumped on the Cain train.

"In my head, I was on the guy," Reynolds said. "I thought he was a special player. The tools were phenomenal, even though he was really crude. But everybody saw him because he was on the team with another guy [Haynes]. But if you didn't know Cain, if you didn't get to spend time with him, you didn't know he had that special work ethic and all of that. And so I had an unfair advantage. I knew the kid at that point."

Many legends have unsolved mysteries baked into them, things that happen that seem to defy explanation, and this is the point of this tale where one comes into play. Sure, Cain was raw, but he performed well at Diamond Club, which is scouted by all 30 teams. He played on a team with a legitimate prospect in Haynes, one who was definitively on the draft radar. How on earth did no one but Reynolds see Cain for more than what he appeared to be?

While Reynolds saw Cain as projectable, one possible reason was that, according to Haynes, his friend didn't pass the "eye test."

"When you walk up to the field and see this guy with a 13 size shoe, he's got the Walmart Wilson on his hand, you're going to say, 'Nah, there's no way,'" Haynes said with a laugh. "He's skinny, his uniform is slightly falling off. He did not look the part; he did not pass the eye test. And then you'd see him do some of the stuff he did and you're like, 'Shoot, if the light switch comes on, it's going to be scary.' But I think it was kind of hit or miss."

The other possible explanation? Geography. Madison County is really far north, right at the start of Florida's Panhandle. It was not where most Florida scouts were located. So even if they were coming to see Haynes, it wasn't a regular stop for area scouts, let along crosscheckers or scouting directors.

"The way Florida works for scouting, most of the guys that have the panhandle, that's a long ways away from home, so they do a trip up to that region once or twice," Reynolds said. "If he was in Tampa, it may have been a little different, he might have gotten a lot more looks. I don't know how many people were on him. I could see how you could think he was just too far away, let him go to school. My guess is that's what a lot of people saw at the time, but I got lucky."

One person who is fairly certain Reynolds is the *only* scout to have even turned Cain in is Ryan Robinson, whose name was mentioned by just about everyone interviewed for this chapter. Robinson was a longtime scout for the Pirates, Angels, and eventually the Brewers, who now runs a travel-ball organization out of Tallahassee called Next Level Baseball while working in the insurance industry as his "day job."

Like many who came in contact with Cain as a high schooler, Robinson's connection came via Jeremy Haynes. Haynes would travel to Tallahassee to work with Robinson on a regular basis and Cain started coming with him. The pair, really the trio, forged a very strong bond, one that continued through the players' times at Tallahassee Community College. Robinson had never seen a young player, especially one so new to the game, with so much desire to improve.

"He was incredible; he was the most driven kid I had ever been around," Robinson said. "The thing about Lorenzo, he never learned the wrong way, he never played travel baseball. He only knew the things in the game of baseball that Barney Myers, Jeremy Haynes, and myself were telling him. He didn't have a lot of outside noise or influences in his life. His internal toughness, his drive, it's better than anybody I've ever seen. None of it, from Madison County to TCC to early in his minor league career, none of it was easy. A lesser kid would've quit during the journey."

Reynolds kept close tabs on Cain over the course of his senior season and saw the tireless work really starting pay off. He was a player who was improving by the day and closing that learning and experience gap. There was one thing he could do, perhaps innately, that gave the veteran area scout more confidence that Cain had the chance to do something at the next level. Remember that Clint Eastwood movie *Trouble with the Curve*? It turned out the prized prospect just could not read breaking stuff, an ailment that has derailed more than one hitter's career. Well, Cain didn't have it.

"He could track a breaking ball," Reynolds said. "You go see raw players in high school and kids like him get a lot of breaking balls and it's swing and miss, swing and miss. Cain could track the breaking ball all the way from the beginning. I don't know if that's an acquired thing or you're born with it, but he had it and he [had it throughout his career], you know? So that made me feel good about him, that he was going to get to contact and he had that sneaky power."

Reynolds had some backup within the organization when it came time to vouch for Cain. Bobby Heck was heading towards his fourth draft as the Brewers' East Coast crosschecker in 2004, after coming over from the Texas Rangers in the fall of 1999. He would go on to become the scouting director of the Houston Astros and a special assistant to the general manager for the Tampa Bay Rays in a long and very successful scouting career.

He gives all of the scouting credit to his area scout, Reynolds, pointing out that not only did he do a fantastic job evaluating

Cain, but also went above and beyond in getting Cain and Haynes to the Diamond Club event, even having the pair stay with him at the showcase. That was the first time Heck heard anything about Cain and it wasn't until midway through the spring of 2004, when he was making his swing through the Panhandle with Reynolds, that he finally laid eyes on him.

"You could just see how interesting of an athlete he was," Heck said. "There was life to his body and pretty innate baseball instincts for someone that hadn't played too often."

While Reynolds put in a good report on Cain, and Heck echoed the sentiment, albeit on just the one look, it wasn't like Cain was going to be considered as an early-round pick. It didn't seem like there were other teams all that interested and while he was catching up to his peers, his lack of baseball résumé made it seem pretty clear he wasn't ready for pro ball.

It's a tough balance to strike as a scout. You might really like a player but understand that he's far away from being able to handle the rigors of that next level. Reynolds had seen plenty of raw players like Cain get chewed up and spit out by the professional game, never getting past the lower levels. He did not want that to happen to Lorenzo Cain.

From the get-go, Reynolds viewed Cain as someone who could be taken as a "draft-and-follow." It was a tool the Brewers liked to use with players like this. Back then, a team had until just before the following year's draft to sign a player after taking him. So with a raw high school talent, a team might select him in a later round then send him off to a junior college to watch how he developed that spring while playing at a higher—but hopefully not overwhelming—level. When the signing deadline was moved to the same summer as the draft with the new Collective Bargaining Agreement in 2007, the draft-and-follow disappeared. It returned, albeit in an altered state, following the 2022 lockout and new agreement that spring.

"This is the perfect candidate, he hasn't played enough base-ball, he's not ready, you can't send him out yet," said Reynolds about his thought process. "He needs more time. It's all tools and makeup and work ethic. Who's to say what would have happened if we had signed him out of high school? Sometimes you're not ready.

"I read his report a few years back and believe it or not I had him in as a 50 [on the 20-to-80 scouting scale], which is ridiculous. I remember seeing that and thinking, 'I had him as a 50 as a draft-and-follow?' You can say how in the world can you [recommend] not to sign a guy that you're saying is an everyday player in the big leagues? But the draft-and-follow was only because I knew he wasn't ready, not because I didn't think he was going to be really good."

———————

Prior to the 2004 Draft, the Brewers tried to line up their premium choices for draft-and-follows and would rank them, guys they wanted to try to beat the rest of the industry to by taking in the top 20 rounds, rather than wait for too long. Reynolds had pushed for Cain to be on that list and, as luck would have it, was invited into the draft room for the first time in his career, as scouting directors will often invite a select group of area guys into the "war room" each year. So Reynolds could, presumably, pound the table for Cain in person. He just couldn't do it too loudly.

"You're not allowed to talk to Jack," Reynolds recalled with a laugh, referring to the scouting director, Jack Zdurencik. "Jack would lose it probably during the draft if you came over and talked to him as an area scout."

So any advocacy from Reynolds had to be relayed through Heck, who had permission to discuss each round's selection with the director. The draft had started with the Brewers taking a pair of high school pitchers, Mark Rogers from Maine and Yovani Gallardo from Texas. Both would go on to reach the big leagues, with Gallardo spending a dozen years there while injuries limited Rogers to a couple of cups of coffee.

Reynolds bided his time, knowing that the sweet spot would probably come towards the end of the day, which ran through 20 rounds back then. He didn't speak up until they took David Johnson out of UCLA (Johnson made it as high as Triple-A but never made it to the big leagues) in Round 15.

"I got up and went over to Bobby as soon as we took a senior sign," Reynolds said. "I went over and said, 'Can we please take Cain now? We're taking guys we don't like and Cain's a 50!'"

Cain wasn't the only high schooler the Brewers were looking at as a potential draft-and-follow at this part of the draft, and Heck was very cognizant of that. Darren Ford, a speedy outfielder from southern New Jersey, was also on that list, and trying to feel out when the right time to take either or both of them was an inexact science, something he discussed with Zdurencik after Reynolds nudged him a little.

"I think it was really the art part of it, where you feel a lull as far as the talent level," Heck said. "And we had multiple guys we wanted to take. You didn't want to push it to the last round just in case someone else had the same idea. So when we felt, 'Hey, the draft is getting a little soft right now. Let's not lose these guys. Maybe now's the time where we can take a couple of them.'"

"Now" turned out to be the 17th round for Cain. The Brewers took a Canadian high school right-hander by the name of Alex Periard, who maxed out in Double-A, the round after they took Johnson. Then they pulled Cain's card, with the fifth selection of Round 17, not quite 20 selections in front of Haynes, who was taken, as a pitcher, by the Red Sox.

Leading up to the draft, there was virtually no communication between Reynolds, the Brewers, or Cain. During the spring, Reynolds mostly stayed in touch with Barney, the coach, to check in if other teams were sniffing around at all. But it largely played out the way Jack Zdurencik preferred: under a shroud of secrecy.

"We didn't want anybody to know anything," Reynolds said. "This was part of Jack's culture… if we can keep it under wraps. I was getting all the information I needed from the coaches there and the only thing I could ruin it with was by telling Cain too much."

The only problem with this philosophy in this situation was that Cain didn't really know very much at all about how baseball beyond high school worked. He hadn't gotten much college attention—Albany State, an HBCU in Georgia, had expressed a little interest, but that was about it. At that point in time, playing pro ball wasn't exactly front and center in his mind.

"I was playing summer ball and my coach said, 'Hey, your buddy just got drafted,'" Haynes recalled. "We had no clue the draft was even that day, he had no idea he got drafted until they called him. And then 20 picks later, or whenever it was, my name gets called. So it was cool to see two guys from a small town make it happen."

When Reynolds called Cain to tell him he had been taken by the Brewers in the 17th round, Cain had a typical, low-key reaction, according to Reynolds.

Reynolds: Cain [everyone called him by his last name at the time], it's Doug Reynolds with the Brewers.

Cain: Hey Coach. [Cain called Reynolds "Coach" ever since he coached him at that Diamond Club event].

Reynolds: We just drafted you in the 17th round. Congratulations.

Cain: Alright.

Click.

Cain perhaps didn't know exactly what being drafted meant; he certainly didn't understand the draft-and-follow, so news that the Brewers had taken him without any context likely wasn't meaningful to him in the moment. It obviously would change his live forever.

———

Being taken as a draft-and-follow and finding a place to go so the team can follow your progress are two different things. At least by the time he hung up on Reynolds, he did have a commitment to go to Tallahassee Community College, once again relying on a little help from his friends.

Haynes initially committed to go to Florida State after high school, but had decommitted prior to the draft and, largely because Robinson coached at TCC, had opted to head to the nearby two-year school. It happened organically that Cain followed his friend to play for the Eagles.

Once again, the young outfielder was hit with a learning curve and once again he had to push through some adversity. He didn't get to TCC and take over the Panhandle Conference by storm. He learned pretty quickly that he had a lot to learn.

It wasn't from a lack of effort. From the get-go, he, Haynes, and Robinson would meet at the gym every morning at around 5:30 AM. Then they would spend time in the cage hitting. Cain was determined to catch up as quickly as possible.

"By 8:00 AM, he had done more than other kids in the country did all day," Robinson said. "And that was before other kids were waking up. He didn't have to do it, he wasn't mandated to do it, he wouldn't have gotten in trouble if he hadn't done it. It's what he wanted to do."

Even with all of that extra work, things didn't start out well. Call it a slump, call it growing pains. Whatever it was, Cain did not produce particularly well in the early stages of the spring of 2005, not terribly surprising given how little baseball he had actually played in his life to that point.

"You just took a kid that started three years ago, he ends up here, he ends up starting in center field," Haynes said. "A lot of things he's not… they start to add up at that level, especially in that area. That Panhandle Conference was tough. You could see where he started kind of spinning his wheels."

It was rough enough early on that Tallahassee coach Mike McLeod, who ran the TCC baseball program from 1990 until retiring after the end of the 2022 season, thought about sitting him. Not surprisingly, word got to Reynolds. Not only did he have his ear to the ground and relationships with just about every coach in his area, but it was McLeod who gave Reynolds his first college coaching job after he was done with his playing career. So Reynolds talked to McLeod and Robinson regularly to check on Cain's progress, along with coming to see him when he could.

"He was awful at the beginning," Reynolds said. "He was scuffling to the point where McLeod said they might not play him. You don't want to hear that about your draft-and-follow. You're not going to get him any money if he doesn't get better."

To his credit, McLeod stuck with his center fielder and, like he did in high school, Cain started to steadily improve. By the end of the spring, he was arguably the best hitter in the conference and he largely erased that slow start to finish with a .319 average and 10 steals in 35 games.

"He just got better, fast," Reynolds said. "I remember [long-time scout] Joe Mason used to say, 'Smooth gets better, faster.' Cain has always been smooth and he just got so much better, so fast."

"Hats off to who he's always been," Haynes said. "He never stopped smiling, he's always competitive. And then, all of a sudden, that light switch came on. You just saw him do stuff and you're like, 'He's got a chance. That light switch has come on and he's going to be special.'"

This is—to flip Reynolds' words around—what a team *does* want to see from a draft-and-follow, even if it is going to cost the team money. Reynolds and Heck were certain they wanted to sign him and there was confidence they could get something done, especially given the area scout's relationship with the player. But they really wanted their boss, Jack Zdurencik, to see Cain before they made a run at signing him.

Zdurencik had never laid eyes on Cain to this point, not uncommon for a scouting director and a later-round pick. But with the junior college season waning—TCC's schedule ended in late April of 2005—Reynolds got his boss to come down. Zdurencik, who would have the ultimate say on what the Brewers could pay Cain, was more than happy to oblige. While he always had supreme faith in his scouts, he also wouldn't want to sign a check sight unseen.

By this point, Cain was in a groove and he put on a good show in front of Zdurencik and Reynolds. Jack Z wanted to see more, so Reynolds arranged a workout the next day and, according to Reynolds, Cain "put on a show." Ryan Robinson concurs and believes that's what really cemented the start of Cain's Brewers career.

"Doug threw Cain BP when Jack was there and, in my opinion, that's kind of when Lorenzo Cain 'arrived,'" Robinson said. "This sounds crazy, but in one BP session, hitting balls halfway up the light standards, it went from being a maybe to being a done deal that the Brewers were going to sign him. If he had a bad BP, maybe they let him go back to the draft and who knows what happens?"

The Brewers had about a month from the end of the TCC season until the deadline to sign Cain or have him go back into the 2005 Draft. That's what happened to Haynes, who ended up not signing with the Red Sox and going much later in that '05 Draft as a pitcher, to the Angels, the team Robinson was scouting for. Haynes and Cain thought they'd both end up back at Tallahassee for their sophomore years together until the Brewers got him signed.

"We just didn't know," Haynes said. "We never really had a feel for how it was supposed to go. I think after the season we thought we'd probably be back and the next thing you know, he signed a contract in his living room and a day later, he's on a plane to Arizona. Everything just kind of happened."

———

It wasn't quite as quick as that. One potential stumbling block was that there were other players the organization wanted to sign. Remember Darren Ford, the speedy New Jersey high schooler the Brewers were also eyeing as a draft-and-follow? Milwaukee had taken him one round after Cain and watched him have a very good year at Chipola Junior College, also in the Florida Panhandle. The Brewers would need $200,000 to get him signed and it's not like they were the Yankees or Dodgers in terms of the ability to spend.

"We were Milwaukee, we weren't throwing money around a lot," Zdurencik said. "But this was a case where there was a lot of conviction on him. Bobby Heck was sold on him and Doug Reynolds really, really wanted him. All I had to do was come in and okay the dollars."

Had he seen Cain not perform well, would he have given the go-ahead? Zdurencik, who would eventually go on to become the general manager of the Seattle Mariners, is pretty certain he would have.

"I always thought that if a scout was convicted, then that player had to be worth something," Zdurencik said. "It was just a matter of how much is that player worth and how much are you willing to go with the scout dollar-wise? How much more are you willing to go above what he originally thought he could sign him for?"

Now, nearly two decades later, there's some disagreement as to how Reynolds entered Cain's TCC apartment living room and delivered the club's opening offer to Cain, his mother, and his uncle. Zdurencik recalls that Reynolds told him he thought he could get it done for around $50,000–$60,000. Reynolds claims that his boss would send you into the house with a low number, one that would be tough to ask for, though he understood it was a way for a smaller-market team to sign more players.

Wherever it originated, Reynolds gritted his teeth and put a $60,000 offer on the table. The general rule of thumb in Jack Zdurencik's scouting department was that you didn't leave the house without a signed contract. But this is where another possible obstacle came into play.

In the very same 2004 Draft, the Mariners had taken their own draft-and-follow in Michael Saunders (out of the British Columbia high school ranks in Canada) and followed his progress at Tallahassee Community College. Saunders would get close to $250,000 to sign with Seattle and there's a chance that Cain, and Cain's mother, knew about that number. At the time, Saunders was considered a more polished player, and he had gone six rounds earlier, in the 11th. Reynolds remembered the Cain contingent wanting $200K to sign. Reynolds called his boss.

"I called and said, 'Jack, you have to give me permission to leave,'" Reynolds said. "Cain's mom was real mad at me and I didn't want to get her so mad at me that he wouldn't sign. I asked him to let me go home and we could talk about it tomorrow."

Zdurencik initially okayed the move, but then called his scout back and told him to return and take the family out to dinner. That didn't go exactly as planned, but Reynolds did get back in Cain's mother's good graces when he returned and asked—after

Zdurencik gave the go-ahead—if $100,000 would get it done. Eventually, Cain would sign officially for $95,000, with $5,000 put aside for college money.

"We gave him more than we thought we were going to give him, but not anywhere near what he was ultimately worth," Zdurencik said.

————

That summer, Cain was part of an outfield in the rookie-level Arizona League with 2005 draftee Michael Brantley, another future All-Star. The pair would get a late promotion up to Helena, in the Pioneer League, and would play alongside the aforementioned Ford, who would touch the big leagues in 2010 and 2011. It was Cain, though, who would be named MVP of the Arizona League after hitting .356/.418/.566 in 50 games there.

There were other struggles along the way, adversity he pushed through in typical Lorenzo Cain style. He'd make his big league debut in July 2010, more than five years after signing with the Brewers. He made his first All-Star team and won his World Series ring with the Kansas City Royals but returned to Milwaukee to finish out his career. He earned over $100 million, putting that draft signing bonus to shame and leaving the kid who didn't know which hand to put the glove on way behind him. His 38.4 career WAR puts him fourth among all players signed from the 2004 Draft, with only one first-rounder (future Hall of Famer Justin Verlander) ahead of him.

"It's not shocking because I know him," Haynes said. "But when you see somebody come from what his starting point was? Yes, that's shocking. But then you think about the competitor, the drive, you start checking off those boxes, you know what he's always been capable of. It's impressive. What he's done over the years, from where he started to where he is now, is pretty cool."

Chapter 8

Albert Pujols

On Friday, September 23, 2022, Albert Pujols homered twice against the Los Angeles Dodgers. This alone wouldn't be anything all that meaningful, considering the future Hall of Famer hit 20 or more homers against 17 other organizations. But these were home runs No. 699 and 700 in his illustrious career, putting him in the very select company of two players (along with Hank Aaron) to have both 700 homers and 3,000 hits.

But beyond the numbers, otherworldly as they might be, there's one indelible image that really stands out from that historic night. When Pujols hit his 699th home run, he watched it for a second, dropped his bat, and rounded the bases quietly. But when No. 700 left his bat, all stoicism left the building and Pujols' home run trot featured a huge smile and the kind of unadulterated joy typically reserved for our youth.

Passing a momentous statistical plateau isn't the end all, be all for a career, obviously. It's not like Pujols' career would have been any less remarkable had he finished shy of the 700 club. There was a weight on Pujols' back, a chip on his shoulder built over the years from all the work he put in to get to that point, from all the sacrifices his family made to bring him to the United States as a teenager, from the transition from the Dominican Republic to the Midwest he had to make in high school, from the sting of being overlooked by the vast majority of the scouting industry and not being taken until Round 13 (pick No. 402 overall) by the St. Louis Cardinals. And he's carried all that for more than two decades. But all of it vanished in that moment of glee as he made his ebullient trip around the bases.

"I wanted to prove to scouts that they were wrong, [as were] the teams that said they were going to draft me and didn't," Pujols said earlier in September of his final big league season in 2022, when the home run tally sat at 695. "When you make it to this level and you had the success you had, yes, you use that. And even now, 23 years later in this game, I still use it.

"But I think I use it to remind me where I came from, not to really show people that they were wrong. I use it right now to remind me of the hard work I had to go through and put in day in and day out. That's something I can apply in my life and my career and help players now."

———————

José Alberto Pujols Alcántara was born in Santo Domingo, the capital of the Dominican Republic. Raised largely by his grandmother, aunts, and uncles, Pujols came from a lower middle class upbringing. He came to the United States in 1996, initially moving to New York city with his grandmother, America, and his father. Because of the combination of a lack of potential job opportunities and concern over safety for the teenager, they moved from New York to Independence, Missouri, a smaller city of about 120,000 people outside of Kansas City, where there were already members of the family who had planted roots.

Moving to the United States at all was hard enough; moving to the heart of the Midwest was more difficult, even with a small Dominican community and family to soften the landing. The 16-year-old had to try to figure out how to fit in without having language to help him.

"I didn't know any English, so it was even tougher for me, even though I had my family there," Pujols recalled. "It was really hard for me because I didn't speak the language. But just like everything else, whatever I put my mind into, I go hard after and give everything. And that's what I did for three months, taking classes three times a week to make sure. Reading books, the dictionary, whatever it took to help me to understand. And even now, 24 years being in the States, I'm still learning the language. There are some words where my pronunciation doesn't come out the way that I want it to. But I was able to understand enough to communicate in high school. And my second year in high school, I was able to take classes by myself. And it was hard. I don't want to tell you it was easy, but nothing that we want to accomplish on this earth is easy."

What did make it easier, of course, was baseball. Pujols, who had been playing in the Dominican against players older than he was, knew he wanted to play the game for as long as he could. He tried out for the Fort Osage High School team in Independence and he obviously became one of the team's standouts quickly. It was that spring that Pujols was noticed by someone outside of the school program for the first time and the fact that American Legion coach Gary Stone saw him play greatly altered the trajectory of his baseball career.

American Legion baseball was created in the United States in 1925 and exists throughout the country. Think of it as a community-based and focused summer ball program. It's not like the travel ball programs we see today, which were just starting to explode when Stone first saw Pujols play in 1997, where you can bounce from team to team. Generally speaking, if you signed on to play with your local American Legion team, you played with them for the entirely of that summer, from Opening Day through the postseason.

Fort Osage was the home base high school for Stone's Post 340 club and he had been tipped off the school had a new student athlete from the Dominican Republic. He went and checked him out and even though Pujols made a few errors that first game, Stone was all in.

"A rival team came up to me and said, 'If you want to release him, I'll take him,'" said Stone, who has spent five decades involved with American Legion baseball and still serves as the National American Legion Baseball Committee chairman. "I said, 'No, that's not going to happen. I don't care how many errors he made, that kid can play.'"

It wasn't just how Pujols swung the bat or the fact that he was already big and strong and looked like a man amongst boys. Stone just liked the way he carried himself, on and off the field, and couldn't wait to invite him to play for him that summer. Pujols committed right away, even though his English still wasn't very good.

"To play this game, you don't need the language," Pujols said. "You know how to play baseball, you know the rules, you know how to run the bases…. The only thing is just the communication, so sometimes we used signs and stuff like that. If you know the signs, you don't need the language really to play the game of baseball. So that took care of itself."

As Pujols was working to learn the language, Stone would ask another member of the team, who happened to be his new player's cousin, to translate. It was the start of a two-year run for Pujols with Post 340 that started to put him on the map a little bit. Stone estimates the young infielder—Pujols played shortstop for his high school and American Legion teams—played in about 120 games, hit 85 home runs, drove in over 250 runs and hit a combined .580.

There are two stories from Pujols' American Legion days that provide some insight into the kind of dedicated and disciplined professional he would eventually become. The first came after that first summer. As word of his dominant performance spread, the travel ball teams came calling. And while Pujols would eventually play a little bit with some teams here and there, he told all interested parties that he was staying put.

"What he told them was that he had committed to Gary Stone and American Legion and that's where he was staying," Stone said proudly. "All these travel teams tried to get him and he said no. He stayed with us."

It was the first time Pujols was able to test his mettle against a higher level of competition and he wasn't about to walk away from the commitment he'd made.

"If you give me the opportunity, I don't care how bad we are, how good we are, I'm going to be loyal to you," Pujols said. "And I was always loyal to Gary Stone and Post 340 because they were good to me. They were the ones that gave me that chance and opportunity.

"I was playing with some of the best players in the Kansas City area and the competition was a little bit different. We had some of the best players for Post 340. We were one game away from winning everything. You build relationships, you pretty much played with the same guys you played with and against in high school. It was pretty awesome."

Pujols still feels indebted that Stone helped him navigate through the language, all while providing rides and equipment when needed.

"You look at my career, 22 years in the big leagues, there are a lot of pieces that had to go right for me to have that success and I believe everything started with high school, with American Legion ball."

It might be hard to imagine Pujols mouthing off or running afoul of a coach, given how he carried himself as a professional.

But the second story does involve one time where Pujols got into trouble.

It was at an American Legion tournament about 80 miles away from Independence. Stone regularly drove Pujols and his cousin to and from these events. Pujols had become a leader on the team and a coach on the field, often positioning his teammates. One game, he and the left fielder got into an argument coming off the field and almost got into a fight. Stone benched both players.

On the ride home, Pujols and his cousin were having an animated conversation in Spanish. After some time had passed, Stone asked Pujols, whose English had rapidly improved by that point, to translate.

Pujols: He said you're stupid.

Stone: Okay. Why?

Pujols: He says I'm the best player on the team and you shouldn't bench me.

Stone: What's your response?

Pujols: I should not fight with my teammates. You should bench me.

"That's a 17-year-old kid saying that," Stone said. "That kind of gives you a little bit of insight into his character."

"I think that was the first time I was ever benched for acting some way I shouldn't," Pujols said. "You're so young and you learn from those mistakes. Part of that allowed me to be a better person and a better teammate."

Following the 1998 high school season, Pujols was ready for a bigger challenge, beyond American Legion ball. He didn't make all of the rounds on the high school showcase that top prospects for the following year's draft often make, but Fernando Arango, a scout at the time for the Tampa Bay Devil Rays, did take Pujols to play in the Area Code Games in California. Arango, who died in 2019, would become a key figure in Pujols' life, not just during the draft process.

"You weren't just seeing the best players in the area; now you're seeing the best players around the nation," Pujols said. "It was fun. The competition was great. For me, I was always loving the competition. I was always excited to compete against the best. I never had any intimidation about playing with the best."

Not being intimidated doesn't mean he necessarily put himself on the map with a strong performance at the event. Scouts who saw him felt he struggled against the better level of pitching.

"We had his name because of Fernando Arango but didn't know a whole lot about him," said longtime scout Dan Jennings, who was the Rays scouting director then. "He didn't do truly anything at the Area Codes that jumped out to grab you. It was lukewarm."

Still, Pujols had put himself on some radars and area scouts were ready to follow him for what was slated to be his senior year of high school at Fort Osage. Instead, Pujols would finish up high school in December so he could start the next chapter and take on the challenge of better competition by heading to junior college ahead of the 1999 Draft.

––––––––

Chris Mihlfeld was the head coach at Metropolitan Community College–Maple Woods who initially recruited Pujols, or perhaps it was Pujols who recruited the school. He knew he wouldn't get evaluated by scouts well at Fort Osage High after getting walked routinely the previous spring. Player and team found each other in the fall of 1998. Maple Woods had made it to the Junior College World Series in its last season, and played games against travel ball teams in the region. One of those teams was run by Dave Bingham, the former head coach at Kansas University, a team that Pujols played for that fall.

It seemingly was a match made in heaven, and Pujols and Mihlfeld remained friends for years, with Mihlfeld serving as Pujols' trainer for more than a decade. But the coach left in December of 1998 to become the strength and conditioning coach for the Los Angeles Dodgers. His assistant, Marty Kilgore, took over and had Albert Pujols dropped in his lap as the slugger really wanted to stay close to family, still a bit intimidated by the size of the country and the idea of going out of state for school. Besides, he already had dreams of pro ball and knew he'd be eligible for the draft that spring, rather than have to wait three years had he gone to a big, four-year school program.

Kilgore knew a little something about grinding it out and getting somewhere when people weren't noticing you. He had played at Longview Community College and then walked on as a pitcher at Iowa State. He coached at Longview, in a volunteer capacity, for eight years, while working to get his college degree. And when he didn't get the Maple Woods head coaching job, a gig Mihlfeld landed, he signed on to be the pitching coach, so he was in the right place at the right time.

"Timing is everything," said Kilgore, who has been Maple Wood's head coach ever since he took over from Mihlfeld, recording over 600 wins in his tenure.

The new coach and Pujols met for the first time in January of 1999. And the future Hall of Famer asked a very simple question: How would Kilgore make him a better hitter?

Kilgore, the former pitching coach who had just become a head coach for the first time in his life, gulped.

"I'm a pitching guy," Kilgore said. "I reverted back to how I was going to get him out as a pitcher, not how I could help him as a hitter, because I knew I couldn't help him as a hitter. I was pretty insecure. I had volunteered for eight years. I didn't know if I could do it. I kind of hid my insecurities and worked like how I had seen other guys do it successfully. I felt like there was a bar to get to, we'd been to the World Series before and I felt like I had to keep doing that."

Having seen Pujols in those fall games, Kilgore knew he would help the school in that lofty goal. And it turned out they had something very important in common: a seemingly tireless work ethic.

Mihlfeld had helped build up the Maple Woods program in a hurry, installing an incredibly thorough workout and practice regimen for the team. Kilgore carried it forward, and to this day scouts credit him with having the hardest working players in the area.

Perhaps that's why it was such a good fit for Pujols in the end. Now everyone knows his work ethic was otherworldly, the main reason why he was able to play as long as he did for as well as he did. Kilgore saw it early in terms of just how tireless he was in terms of working on his offensive game.

"I've never been around a guy who cared that much, worked so hard," Kilgore said. "We hit three times a day. I've been fortunate enough to coach four guys who made it to the big leagues. I've seen guys who have had the work ethic that Albert had, but didn't have the talent. I've never been around anybody that had the complete package. That confidence, that ability. He knew that he deserved an opportunity to play at a high level, at a professional level."

———

Kilgore knew he had a special player, but he didn't know how much the scouting industry would pay attention. He started to get a sense, he said, when at the start of the season he came down to breakfast at the hotel the team was staying at and saw close to two dozen scouts there as well.

They likely weren't all there to see Pujols. Reports say that first game of Pujols' junior college career came against left-hander Mark Buehrle. Buehrle was in his second season at Jefferson College in Hillsboro, Missouri, and had been taken in the 38th round of the 1998 Draft by the Chicago White Sox. He was a "draft and follow," so the White Sox had control over Buehrle all spring. He would pitch so well that spring the White Sox would sign him for $150,000 and he would go on to win over 200 games, make five All-Star teams, and win a World Series.

Scouts in the area would obviously clamor over getting to see Buehrle face a tough opponent, and to see how Pujols would fare against that caliber of pitching. To get that kind of JUCO matchup early on does not happen often.

Reports say Pujols got the better of the left-hander, hitting a grand slam in the opener. It was the start of a ridiculously productive year at the plate for Pujols, who would hit .466 with 22 homers and 76 RBIs in 56 games, leading Maple Woods to a Region 16 Championship and earning a spot on the NJCAA All-American team.

But while scouts were there on the regular, he obviously wasn't seen as a slam-dunk early pick. Not every scout loved the swing, thinking it was long at times, though no one could refute the tremendous strength and raw power. Pujols was already a mature young adult, and didn't hang out with his teammates, choosing rather to spend time with the coaching staff. He didn't live on or right near campus with other players. That, along with a language barrier that existed despite Pujols' efforts to learn English, caused some scouts to view him as a bit aloof or distant. More than anything, though, the concerns scouts voiced were about his body, or lack thereof.

Scouting players can be a merciless business, and sometimes draft prospects can be described more as cattle than human beings. But when you're in the business of trying to project what a player could become down the road, evaluations on body type are important. And Pujols, at age 19 in junior college, would have classified as a "bad body" player who was seen as a bit soft.

Even those who liked his bat and strong arm worried about his conditioning. They knew he wouldn't stay at shortstop, where he played in high school and at Maple Woods. Could he play third? If his body went south as he matured, would he be limited to first base only at a young age? If so, that would scare off many evaluators. Right-handed hitting, right-handed throwing first baseman is a tough profile and it puts even more pressure on the bat to be special.

In today's game, perhaps a hitter like Pujols would not have slipped through the cracks like he did. Data like exit velocity and launch angle certainly would have helped him. Frankly, he might have been seen more and given more opportunities as a high schooler. Maybe area scouts in the Midwest wouldn't have been quite as perplexed as what to do with a Latino player who looked like a man amongst the boys.

Whatever the reasons, while Pujols' games were regularly attended, there just wasn't buzz generating. There were teams who turned in reports on him and area scouts who liked him, at least to a certain degree. There were the Red Sox, with new part-time scout Ernie Jacobs a fan of Pujols' power. The Mets had interest thanks to area scout Larry Chase. The aforementioned Arango, with the Rays, likely turned in the highest report on him. And of course there was Cardinals' area scout Dave Karaff, the man who would eventually win the draft equivalent of the Mega Millions Lottery. Pujols tried to keep all of that out of his mind as much as he was able.

"At the end of the day, I know I couldn't control what happened in the seats," said Pujols about the interest from scouts. "All I could control is what happened on the field and myself. So I was always focusing on doing my work and doing my job and let that take care of itself. Let my work and my job talk for me. I have never really focused on the things that people say or stuff I cannot control."

————

Now's the time in the story to try and separate fact from fiction, urban legend from what really happened. Invariably with a player like this, hindsight will create tons of scouts who swear up and down that they turned in a good report on Pujols, but their team didn't take him. Or that they even pounded the table for him only to get turned away.

Doing as much sleuthing as possible, here is what seems to have occurred as the spring of 1999 went on and the draft approached.

Those area scouts, and some others, turned in reports on Pujols, with varying degrees of support for potential at the next level. Some teams never sent in a cross-checker to see him. Some crosscheckers came in and didn't like what they saw, so they wouldn't be the ones to go to the mat in the draft room should his name have come up. And if he wasn't crosschecked, or those higher-level scouts didn't like him, he may not have been on that many draft boards.

Jacobs told the *Boston Globe* in 2006 that he turned him in as a third- or fourth-round-caliber player and tried to get scouting director Wayne Britton to send a crosschecker in. Never happened.

"I rang the bell all year, 'Come see this kid,'" Jacobs told the *Globe.* "Wayne didn't send anybody in. I think what happened was, this was my first full year as a scout, and Albert didn't make the airplane talk [scouts, crosscheckers, who fly in to see players]. There were a couple of scouts who liked him, who thought he could go high, but there were a lot that didn't."

Even without the crosschecking, the Red Sox came close to taking Pujols starting around Round 10. But, according to Jacobs' account, a combination of signability concerns—there was talk that Pujols was looking for somewhere in the $100,000–$150,000 range—some conditions the Red Sox had about him signing quickly and Jacobs' not being able to get Pujols on the phone to run through those, they never officially pulled his card.

Pujols said the Mets and Larry Chase, who died in 2012, were interested in taking him around Round 9, but it seems like the signability was a concern there as well. One of the sticking points, even when it came to eventually signing with the Cardinals, says Pujols, was paying for any future education. Yes, he wanted to play baseball professionally. Yes, he had confidence he could make it. But he also knew that there were no guarantees and was apparently adamant that any team taking him should kick in money, around $30,000, for college should things not work out on the diamond.

Then there were the Rays, providing one of the best "the one who got away" stories regarding Pujols—or any player for that matter—even if there are slightly different versions of what happened. There is no question that Arango was very high on Pujols—perhaps more than any other scout in the area—and that he never wavered in his evaluation, no matter how much it flew in the face of what others in the organization thought they saw.

Remember, Arango had brought Pujols out to the Area Code Games and his boss, Dan Jennings, didn't see anything of note at that event. He wasn't alone; other scouts at the Area Codes that summer, even from that area, have the same recollection.

Fast-forward to the spring and Arango is turning in the same reports and Pujols is putting up video game numbers at Maple Woods. To Jennings' credit, he actually sent not one crosschecker, but several, as the spring rolled on. He felt the first one, though he couldn't be sure, might have been Michael Hill, who went on to become GM of the Miami Marlins and now works in the Commissioner's Office. One of the difficulties with crosschecking is that you fly in, see a player one day, and then have to go on to the next guy. Hill didn't see Pujols on a great day and felt he couldn't write him up.

Jennings had a rule, though. If there was a separation of two or more grades between the area scout's reports and any other reports, he would send in another scout to take a look. And it's not like he sent an intern from behind his desk. At different times he sent Stan Meek, who would go on to become the scouting director for the Miami Marlins, and RJ Harrison, who would succeed Jennings and be the Rays' scouting director for a long time as well. And each time, they didn't see what Arango was seeing.

Some of it has to do with timing. Pujols had hit another homer against Buehrle in their regional tournament, though it was a solo shot and Buehrle won the game. Maple Woods would go on to win their region and then play at Seminole State. This was getting to be last-looks time and scouts poured in, with some remembering as many as 40 being in attendance. And on that day, Pujols struck out several times, leaving many scouts departing while shaking their heads.

Still, Arango had him at the top of his list and Jennings didn't want to completely toss that aside. So they arranged for Pujols to come to Tampa for a private workout. Anyone and everyone from the Rays' baseball operations department would attend their pre-draft workouts, including general manager Chuck LaMar. They had Pujols run the 60-yard dash, reported as 7.1 seconds by MLB.com (via an interview with Arango). They worked him out all over the infield, trying to answer the question many scouts had about his defensive home.

"Everything. Shortstop, third base, first base, and behind the plate," Pujols said. "That was the last thing that I did."

It's hard to imagine Pujols as a catcher, and perhaps luckily in terms of the longevity of his career, he didn't stand out too much back there other than showing off a strong arm. Then it came time for what everyone wanted to see, whether you loved him or didn't know what to do with him: batting practice.

This is where the reports start to diverge. There are some that talk about a moon shot off the top of the foul pole. Jennings remembers one fairly non-descript home run in the session.

"He was a deep back-leg guy with kind of an uphill type swing," Jennings said about Pujols' hitting mechanics.

Jennings recalled that the brain trust at the upper levels of the baseball operations department did not have their mind changed by this workout, though Arango kept insisting Pujols should go early. He told both MLB.com and *Baseball America* that he thought Pujols would hit 40 home runs in a major league season one day. "They looked at me like I was crazy," he told MLB.com.

"We tried everything we could to respect the area scout's stance on this player," Jennings said. "After the workout, those of us who were down for the draft go back upstairs and we go over the list. We get to Pujols. 'Fellas, anybody here got something you want to add? Do we need to move this guy up the board? Fernando's still got him number one. We all just saw him.' No one raised their hands. No one said anything. So we kept him where we kept him."

Now, the popular story is that Arango was so upset that the Rays didn't take Pujols he quit a year later. And he did leave the organization, and scouting, for a while, working for an agency before returning to the industry with the Milwaukee Brewers and eventually reuniting with Pujols by working for the Cardinals. But Jennings, who will quickly and readily admit that he was wrong and Arango was right, cries foul when it comes to that legend.

"Those things are not true," Jennings insists. "There was never that jumping up and down, 'Jesus, this is the guy! If you don't take this guy, it's going to be the biggest mistake!' There was never that type of conviction. But he did like him, and he liked him a lot. And it was definitely a mistake by us in Tampa and by 29 other teams, because truthfully, this guy should have been the first player taken by a longshot in any draft."

Sadly, we can't know for certain what Arango's true motivations were now that he is no longer with us. But there are two things that are certain with this intersection of Pujols' life and the Tampa Bay Devil Rays. The first is that Arango and Pujols became chosen family. Pujols didn't come across many scouts, or other people in baseball in the Midwest, who spoke Spanish, and that connection helped the pair bond quickly. It's clear Arango was a bit of a father figure and the first person in professional baseball who truly believed in what Albert Pujols could become.

"I still have a relationship with his wife and his son, Tony," an emotional Pujols said. "God always puts great people in your life. And Fernando was that guy to me. He always encouraged me. It gives me goosebumps. I'm sad because he would've been the guy who would be so happy with everything that's going on with me in my life. Although I shared a lot of those moments with him when he was alive, I do miss him."

The other certainty is that Dan Jennings changed the way he ran his drafts. He looks wistfully back at 1999 and recognizes that after getting Josh Hamilton No. 1 overall and Carl Crawford in the second round, had he listened to Arango, that could have gone down as one of the best drafts by any team ever. (He also missed on taking Jake Peavy from his own hometown, adding salt to the wound.) And from the time he saw Pujols arrive and take the National League by storm in 2001, he promised to at least try to not make the same mistake twice.

"There's so many years where the draft has splintered by the fifth round, you get six, seven, eight, 10, just call out a guy who's been at the top of a guy's list and you have the chance to look like a genius," Jennings said. "The lesson I learned is that if a scout had the gumption to keep any player that high on his list, no matter how poor the performance was when he was cross-checked, there reached a point in subsequent drafts where I just took the player and I wish like hell it would've started that year."

––––––––

That, of course, leaves the Cardinals. Dave Karaff was the organization's area scout at the time and, truth be told, he didn't file a report filled with lavish praise of Pujols. He thought he had a chance to hit, but like many others, worried a bit about the body. This apparently wasn't anything all that new for Karaff, who rarely was effusive in his evaluations of players in his area.

Perhaps the Cardinals would have crosschecked Pujols anyway. After all, it wasn't all that far from St. Louis. But it certainly didn't hurt that Mike Roberts, a crosschecker with the Cardinals, was also Karaff's brother-in-law. And unlike with the unfortunate series of events that transpired with the Rays, Roberts saw a good version of Pujols and became an advocate, one to whom many give the most credit for the Cardinals finally taking Pujols in Round 13.

Roberts was a very well-respected scout, one who had taken John Mozeliak under his wing a bit. And in 1999, Mozeliak was in his first season as the club's scouting director, working closely with Jeff Scott, who carried the title "director of player procurement." So when Roberts started talking up Pujols as the draft wore on, Mozeliak listened.

"You ask why would I trust Mike Roberts? Well, I trusted him with a lot," said Mozeliak, who would go on to become the Cardinals' general manager and now has the title of president of baseball operations. "And it wasn't just in 1999. It was for the next 15 years or so as well. So here's a man that I had a lot of respect for and thankfully, I had a lot of respect for him in the early years, because, maybe if I didn't, or didn't have that type of trust, we don't have the kind of story we have now."

Also working in the Cardinals' favor was an extra look late in the spring that helped corroborate Karaff's and Robert's opinions. The Cardinals, like most teams, were on hand to see Pujols' poor performance against Seminole State. National crosschecker Clark Crist, who most recently has managed a team in the Appalachian League, told the *Roanoke Times* that he didn't know what to do with Pujols after that first game. But unlike most of the industry who left, Crist came back the next day.

"Sure enough, he hit one a country mile," Crist told the *Roanoke Times*. "It was a beautiful swing."

It's not like these reports catapulted Pujols to the top of the Cards' draft board, otherwise this would be a much different story. Back then, the scouting department would put together a top 100 or 125 players. After that, they would rank remaining players by position and, typically, after they got past the 10th round, they would start looking at some positional needs to fill out rosters. Pujols was, according to Mozeliak, at the top of their third-basemen list in that next tier of players. It came up as the draft hit the double-digit rounds that they did have a need for corner infielders and that eventually led them to taking Pujols. That and Roberts in the draft room placing reminders.

"He was definitely an advocate for him, for sure," Mozeliak said.

"You could argue we didn't get it right," he continued. "Here's a player who ended up, at the time, the greatest hitter on Earth. And you could make the argument he's one of the greatest hitters to ever play. How does he get to the 13th round? We know we were lucky."

And they almost didn't sign him. There was an understanding that there would be some negotiating that would have to take place, and Pujols didn't sign immediately, instead heading to

Hays, Kansas, and the Jayhawk League, a wood-bat college show-case league. As he played there, negotiations were not smooth, though Mozeliak did go see him play for the first time when his team was in the National Baseball Congress World Series in Wichita. Pujols remembers someone in the organization suggest-ing that he be a draft-and-follow. The original offer was reportedly only $10,000. There was a not-insignificant chance that Pujols would spend another season at Maple Woods.

"I was considering going back to school," Pujols said. "It wasn't just a signing bonus. If the Cardinals didn't want to pay for my studies, I wasn't going to sign because education was huge for me. You flip a coin, heads or tails; you don't know if you're going to make it. But one thing you can secure is your education."

"Albert called me. Obviously, he was upset and emotional," his junior college coach Marty Kilgore said. "He said, 'I guess I'm coming back to Maple Woods.'"

To this day, Kilgore can't help but get fired up about how he feels Pujols was treated—or mistreated—by the scouting industry. Years ago, he gave interviews where he did not pull punches on how he felt Midwest scouts had gotten this one wrong. It left a mark deep enough where he chose his words a little more care-fully now, with the additional years adding some wisdom. But the combination of his player not being taken until pick No. 402 and how he felt Pujols was initially treated in negotiations, the old scar comes back to the surface.

"I had scouts here locally that made comments about Albert that were really derogatory, that were not complimentary," Kilgore said. "That really pissed me off. And that's why I said those things about the scouts in general [years ago]. I shouldn't get upset and fired up. But we're going back in history. I haven't gone there in a long, long time."

While Kilgore wears his emotions on his sleeve, Pujols looks back at the time with the grace that perhaps comes at the end of an illustrious and lucrative career. The Cardinals eventually came around and gave Pujols a total of $60,000—a $30,000 signing bonus and $30,000 more for school. He made quick work of the minors, playing there for the 2000 season and then making the big league club in 2001 and never looking back.

The issues with his body? Well, he was already starting to grow into the man baseball fans watched with awe for the past two-plus decades. But this is where his Hall of Fame–caliber work ethic came into play. The Cardinals sat down with Pujols when he was playing in the Arizona Fall League after the 2000 season and told him he needed to get in better shape if he wanted to play in St. Louis. He listened and showed up sculpted and trim for what would be his incredible rookie season. And that he was able to come back to where it all started to get past that home run plateau? It's the stuff legends are made of, and a nostalgic Pujols, while never quite forgetting the slights that fueled him, also has a lot of love for how it all unfolded.

"It's always appreciation," Pujols said. "They didn't have to draft me. And they did. They took a chance; they gave me a chance. I know there were some people who thought I was never going to make it, within the organization, too. I proved them wrong."

Acknowledgments

Ask anyone who has written a book and they'll likely tell you it's a labor of love. And this one, my second, certainly falls under that category. There have been many obstacles over the course of completing this work, from personal- and family-health issues I won't bore you with to the pandemic, which certainly slowed all of us down. There is no way I would have been able to see this project through without a lot of help and support along the way.

That starts with my family. My wife, Sara, has been a consistent presence, from encouraging me to enter the book-writing fray again, to helping make sure I created the space to write. She constantly encourages me to be the best version of myself and to embark on things I care about, with an understanding that challenging myself to take this on was important to me from the get-go.

While I likely won't ever catch up to her in the books published rankings, my mother continues to be a true role model for me in terms of how to conduct myself and excel as a professional and in life. It was her passion for baseball that was passed on to me that created this spark in the first place.

The last time I published a book, my children were seven and four, so the dynamic is obviously a bit different now. My son, Ziv, has taken the love for baseball heirloom and run with it, pitching through college and looking to embark on a career in the sport. He's been a terrific sounding board for the stories I tried to tell here and his excitement about them helped fuel me throughout the process. My daughter Elena's constant support and encouragement, even when she was dealing with her own life, kept me going often when I wanted to stop.

This would get too long if I were to list every scout I talked to for this book. So I'll just thank the entire scouting industry for their tireless work away from the spotlight, their passion for the game, and their willingness to tell their stories so openly and colorfully. My conversations with many of them over the years of my career provided the seeds for this book and I am extremely grateful for their time and patience with me to get their stories right. The same can be said for the many college and high school coaches I spoke to, who made these tales even more robust.

I am extremely thankful for the players, past and present, who agreed to speak to me at length about these origin stories of their careers. Shane Bieber, Charlie Blackmon, Ian Kinsler, Albert Pujols, and Joey Votto were so gracious and I truly appreciate their voices. I hope they enjoyed the conversations as much as I did. Special thanks to Rob Butcher, Josh Goldberg, and Dennis Wyrick among several who helped connect me with players and other interview subjects.

When you head into a collaboration with a publisher, you hope you click with your editor. Jesse Jordan not only got what I was trying to achieve, but also helped me bring it to fruition. Bouncing ideas back-and-forth while being on the same page was truly invaluable, as was his incredible patience and flexibility. That's also true of my agent, Stacey Glick, who brings incredible knowledge of the business and a no-nonsense approach along with incredible kindness and compassion.

Sources

https://etobicokesports.ca/joey-votto/

https://www.mlb.com/news/featured/joey-votto-s-incredible-journey-to-the-reds

https://torontosun.com/2014/06/18/the-joey-votto-legend-grows

https://www.macleans.ca/society/playing-for-keeps/

https://www.orlandosentinel.com/sports/os-jacob-degrom-from-calvary-christian-stetson-to-mets--20150815-story.html

https://nypost.com/2014/08/01/how-jacob-degrom-went-from-light-hitting-ss-to-mets-stud-pitcher/

https://www.masslive.com/redsox/2015/07/what_is_mookie_betts_real_name.html

https://usatodayhss.com/2014/red-sox-call-up-former-overton-star-mookie-betts)

https://www.mainstreetpreps.com/county/davidson/fresh-off-world-series-title-mookie-betts-gets-his-own-day-in-nashville/article_11499034-2533-11eb-a21c-1f7f0c610a4a.html

https://www.mlb.com/news/mookie-betts-rise-to-baseball-star

http://fenwayparkdiaries.com/best%20players/mookie%20betts.htm#:~:text=In%20that%20moment%2C%20Red%20Sox,him%20for%20about%2010%20minutes.

https://www.masslive.com/redsox/2017/02/how_mike_trout_mookie
_betts_we.html

https://www.bostonglobe.com/sports/2015/02/18/neuroscouting-may
-give-red-sox-heads-prospects-potential/EFBHR3zNdThk1N
boRpNMHL/story.html

https://www.masslive.com/redsox/2017/02/how_mike_trout_mookie
_betts_we.html

https://www.theguardian.com/sport/2020/oct/23/mookie-betts-dodgers
-baseball-dunk-bowling-world-series#:~:text=He%20can%20
even%20dunk%2C%20which,you're%20only%205ft%209in.

https://twitter.com/thetshf/status/905166292621156352?lang=en

https://www.mlb.com/news/red-sox-get-world-series-talent-in-2011
-draft-c299729356

https://www.bostonglobe.com/sports/2015/02/18/neuroscouting
-may-give-red-sox-heads-prospects-potential/EFBHR3zNdThk1N
boRpNMHL/story.html

https://www.tallahassee.com/story/sports/local-sports/2014/10/09
/cains-story-continues-spread-mlb-playoffs/16970987/

https://www.espn.com/mlb/story/_/id/9165333/assessing-kansas
-city-haul-zack-greinke

https://www.usatoday.com/story/sports/mlb/2014/10/20/lorenzo-cain
-late-bloomer-kansas-city-royals-world-series/17640339/

https://www.vivaelbirdos.com/st-louis-cardinals-sabermetrics-analysis
/2014/12/26/7450193/albert-pujols-recalling-an-urban-legend
-plus-a-tale-of-two-scouting

https://archive.seattletimes.com/archive/?date=20060524&slug=seam24

https://www.espn.com/mlb/playoffs2006/columns/story?columnist
=thompson_wright&id=2637763

https://tht.fangraphs.com/albert-pujols-revisiting-the-early-years/

https://www.legion.org/baseball/230353/vision-american-legion-baseball

https://www.espn.com/mlb/news/story?id=6189583

https://books.google.com/books?id=J6lbAgAAQBAJ&printsec=front
cover&source=gbs_ge_summary_r&cad=0#v=onepage&q&f=false)

https://www.thepitchkc.com/say-it-aint-steroids/

https://tht.fangraphs.com/albert-pujols-revisiting-the-early-years/

https://roanoke.com/sports/local/mcfarling-pulaski-skipper-clark
-crist-connects-with-baseballs-best/article_1901a0dc-fed0-11ec
-a084-7f7881209df4.html

http://archive.boston.com/sports/baseball/redsox/articles/2006/10/11
/one_that_got_away/

https://www.baseballamerica.com/stories/the-man-who-predicted
-pujols-rise/

https://www.mlb.com/news/albert-pujols-talent-doubted-before-mlb
-draft-c181826188